HOLY GHOST SERMONS

A Living Classic

HOLY GHOST SERMONS

by
Mrs. M. B. Woodworth-Etter

Harrison House
Tulsa, Oklahoma

All Scripture quotations are taken from the *King James Version* of the Bible.

12 11 10 09   10 9 8 7 6 5 4 3 2 1

Holy Ghost Sermons
A Living Classic
ISBN 13: 978-1-57794-160-6
ISBN 10: 1-57794-160-8
Copyright ©1918

Published by Harrison House Publishers © 1997
P.O. Box 35035
Tulsa, Oklahoma 74153
www.harrisonhouse.com

From the Publisher

HOLY GHOST SERMONS BY MRS. M. B. WOODWORTH-ETTER WAS first published in September of 1918. Harrison House is pleased to offer it as a Living Classic Edition. We have reprinted the text almost exactly as it appeared in the original edition which Mrs. Etter compiled and organized herself.

(Capitalization has been stylized. And, for the most part, sentence structure and punctuation have been retained, with words enclosed in brackets added for clarity.)

Readers will best understand Mrs. Etter's message by noting her relationship with God and the time frame in which she ministered. Signs and wonders powerfully earmarked her ministry. And her message is timeless, though some of her language is dated. So please bear in mind that Mrs. Etter spoke and acted upon the revelation she possessed in her day. Her interpretations of Bible prophecy in light of World War I and the evolving technology of her day are most interesting.

We therefore recommend that this book be read in light of present-day revelation from God's Word. The Spirit of the Lord is continually opening the eyes of our understanding to know His mind and ways.

Contents

Preface

IT IS JUST TWO YEARS SINCE I GOT FIFTEEN THOUSAND OF MY LAST, large book "Signs and Wonders" (nearly six hundred pages) off the press....Nearly half of these messengers are now out among the people, testifying to the Signs and Wonders wrought in my ministry through the Name of Jesus. We constantly get wonderful reports from this book.

For some time there has been a great demand for a book with some of my sermons that will meet the needs of the people, in these days of tests, trials, and tribulations. The present day conditions have been seen and prophesied many times in my meetings. These sermons were preached under the anointing of the Spirit, and are especially intended to get God's people SEALED in the SPIRIT unto the Coming of the Lord, so that they will go up with Jesus, when He comes for His bride.

This is my latest work. Under the anointing of the Spirit, I have been enabled to delve into some of the Hidden Mysteries, surrounding the closing of the Gentile Age, and revealing the advent and nearness of the Coming of Jesus.

The Anointing Abides. The work goes on in the newly erected Tabernacle, 2112 Miller Street, West Indianapolis, Indiana.

Lend a helping hand in scattering these white-winged, dove-like messengers of God's truth. Our reward will soon follow us. Amen.

Mrs. M. B. Woodworth-Etter

September 1918

Synopsis of My Early Life
and Experience
in the Work, Condensed

I WAS BORN IN NEW LISBON, OHIO, JULY 22, 1844, AND WAS THE fourth daughter of Samuel Underwood. My parents were not Christians, but when I was ten years old they joined the Disciples' Church. One year later my father, who was a drunkard, got struck by lightning in a terrible storm and died. It was an awful blow to all our young hearts, to see our father carried cold and stiff into the house, and mother fainting as fast as they could bring her to. There were eight of us children, and soon myself and older sisters had to go out and work to provide for the family. I longed for an education, but this seemed impossible. At the age of thirteen I attended a meeting that a Dr. Belding was holding. When I heard the story of the Cross, my heart was filled with the love of Jesus, and my eyes seemed to be a fountain of tears. When the invitation to seek God was given I was the first one to start. It seemed so far to the front, but I said:

> I can't but perish if I go,
> I am resolved to try;
> For if I stay away I know
> I shall forever die.

The minister took a great interest in me and said many things to encourage me. If he could have looked forward and seen my life work for the Master he would have rejoiced to know how kindly he had spoken to the poor little orphan girl. But I did not get fully converted then. The next day as they took me down to the creek to baptize me, I heard some one say: "Maybe she will be drowned." It scared me a little. I thought maybe I will, but I said, Lord, I will go through if I do. So [I] asked the Lord to save me. While going down in the water a light came over me and I was converted. The people saw the change and said I had fainted. Then began my new life of peace and joy in a Savior's love. I also felt that I had a call to go out into the highways and hedges, and gather in the lost sheep.

The church in those days did not believe that women had a right to publicly preach Jesus. Had I told them my heart's desire they would have mocked me.

Later, I married a Mr. Woodworth, and hoped by doing so the way would open that I could go out in the work for Jesus. But one trial and hardship after another was my lot. I felt happy with a few little children that God gave us, but soon the Angel of Death took away my bright, blue-eyed darling boy. One year had hardly passed before another one was taken away. About this time my little daughter, Georgia, was converted. We loved so much to talk about the goodness of God, and longed for the time when we could meet the little ones over on the other shore. In a short time she took sick and died. For weeks before she died her face was all lighted up with the glory of God. She would say: "O mamma, if you could go with me I would be so happy." I said, "Georgia I will try." But that would not do. She said, "Oh mamma, say you will. I cannot die unless you promise to meet me in heaven." I said, "Georgia, by the grace of God I will meet you in heaven." She said, "Now I am ready. I know you will come."

The Sabbath before she died she called me to her bedside and said: "Mamma, I am going to leave you this week," and began to set her house in order. To me she gave her Testament. Just before she passed over she said: "O mamma, I see Jesus and the angels coming for me." It seemed to me that I could see them as they went sweeping through the gates into the New Jerusalem. It was like death to part with my darling, but Jesus was precious to my soul. I could say with David, they cannot come back to me, but I can go to them. Praise the Lord for the Christians' hope.

From the time of the sad occurrences just mentioned my health was very poor. I seemed to hover between life and death many times. Now I know that all this time God was preparing me for my life's work. I could never dismiss the call I had from my mind, and Jesus began to give me such wonderful visions. Heaven is located, its inhabitants are real and not imaginary. I saw Jerusalem in it and talked face to face with Jesus. But I was not willing to go.

When alone I missed my darling so much that I wept as though my heart would break. Then I would always pray; and as I prayed I would forget everything earthly and soar away by faith to the Golden City, and there see my darlings all together shining in glory, and looking at me and saying,"Mamma, do not weep for us, but come this way." I would always end in praising and giving glory to God for taking them to such a happy place. Lizzie, our oldest child, aged sixteen, was all we had left of six sweet children.

In all these trials God was preparing me and opening the way for the great battle against the enemy of souls; and now the great desire of my heart was to work for Jesus. I longed to win a star for the Saviour's crown. But when I thought of my weakness I shrank from the work. Sometimes when the Spirit of God was striving and calling so plainly, I would yield and say,"Yes, Lord; I will go." The glory of God came upon me like a cloud, and I seemed to be carried away hundreds of miles and set down in a field of wheat, where the sheaves were falling all around me. I was filled with zeal and power, and felt as if I could stand before the whole world and plead with dying sinners. It seemed to me that I must leave all and go at once. Then Satan would come in like a flood and say,"You would look nice preaching, being a gazing-stock for the people to make sport of. You know you could not do it." Then I would think of my weakness and say,"No, of course I cannot do it." Then I would be in darkness and despair. I wanted to run away from God, or I wished I could die; but when I began to look at the matter in this way, that God knew all about me, and was able and willing to qualify me for the work, I asked Him to qualify me.

I want the reader to understand that at this time I had a good experience, a pure heart was full of the love of God, but was not qualified for God's work. I knew that I was but a worm. God would have to take a worm to thresh a mountain. Then I asked God to give me the power He gave the Galilean fishermen—to baptize me for service. I came like a child asking for bread. I looked for it. God did not disappoint me. The power of the Holy Ghost came down as a cloud. It was brighter than the sun. I was covered and wrapped up in it. My body was light as the air. It seemed that heaven came down. I was baptized with the Holy Ghost, and fire, and power, which has never left me. Oh, Praise the Lord. There was liquid fire and the angels were all around in the fire and glory. It is through the Lord Jesus Christ and by this power that I have stood before hundreds of thousands of men and women proclaiming the unsearchable riches of Christ.

The time finally came when I felt I had to promise God or die. I promised God that if He would restore my health and show me the work I would do it. I got better immediately. Soon we moved to another settlement, and they took me to church. God seemed to say to me, I brought you here; go to work. I was very timid. When I arose to testify I trembled like a leaf, and began to make excuses, saying: "O God, send some one else." Then the Lord caused me to see the bottomless pit open in all its horror and woe. There was weeping, wailing and gnashing of teeth. It was surrounded by people who seemed unconscious of their danger and without a moment's warning would tumble into this awful place. I was above on a narrow plank walk, which wound up towards heaven, exhorting and pleading with the people to escape that awful place. This vision left a great impression on my mind. In meetings when I felt I should talk or pray I would resist as long as I could; then this awful vision would rise before me, and I would see souls sink into eternal woe. Again I would hear the voice of Jesus whisper, I am with you; be not afraid. In a moment I would be on my feet or knees. I would have been glad to preach had I been a man, and not had so much opposition from my husband and friends.

Several ministers whom I had never seen before told me that God was calling me to the ministry and that I would have to go. Then I thought of going through a course of studies, but could not get my mind on any study. Everything seemed empty and vacant.

In a vision one night Jesus asked me what I was doing on the earth. I said, "I am going to work in Thy vineyard." He said, "When?" I answered, "When I get prepared." Jesus said: "Souls are perishing. Go now and tell the people what I have done for you and I will be with you." I told Him I did not understand the Bible well enough. Then there appeared upon the wall a large open Bible, and the verses stood out in raised letters. The glory of God shone round about the book. I looked and I could understand it all. Then Jesus said again, "Go, and I will be with you." I cried, "Lord, where shall I go?" Jesus said, "Go here, go there, wherever souls are perishing."

The first meeting that I undertook to hold was in a little town among my husband's people, where we had lived before. I said in the Name of the Lord I will try and leave the results with God. As I arose to speak this text came to me: "Set thy house in order, for thou shalt die and not live" (Isaiah 38:1). The timid spirit left me and the words came faster than I could give them utterance. People got converted all through the neighborhood. Soon after this God led me to a place called the Devil's Den. It was distinguished for infidelity and skepticism. There was an old free church there, in which no one was ever known to be converted.

Some of the best ministers had tried to hold meetings here, but left the place in disgust. When I arrived a large crowd came out of curiosity to see me, and expected me to back out. I also appointed day meetings. They said no one will come. I told them if they do not come I will be alone and pray God to pour out His Spirit on the people. God came to my rescue. The fire fell. The news spread like fire, and Christians, singers and ministers came in for miles around. There were hundreds who could not get in the church. An old man, his wife and nine children got converted. Some of the hardest sinners in the whole country got converted. I organized a Sabbath school of one hundred and fifty scholars, and put a man in for superintendent who had been a noted drunkard. From this time forth "Macedonian calls" [See Acts 16:9] came in constantly, and people would fall like dead men and women when the power fell. They would lay for days at a time and have visions and come out brightly converted.

From the early part of my ministry, which is now over forty years, some came out speaking in other tongues. I never felt led to speak much about this experience, but I knew it was of God, and according to the Bible. God also gave me the ministry of healing. He showed me that I was to lay hands on the sick and pray for their recovery. The first person that I laid my hands on publicly and prayed for was instantly healed of an incurable disease, and turned out to be a wonderful worker in the meeting. This gave me hope and courage, and I have now in my ministry prayed for hundreds and thousands of people. People almost innumerable from all walks of life have been healed of all manner of diseases that mankind is akin to. Healing for the body, like salvation for the soul, is in the Atonement, and belongs to the Gospel. They should never be separated. I have traveled the continent many times, and preached to thousands of people in all the large cities of this country. While always weak in the natural, I followed where the Spirit led, and trusted Him for the anointing whenever needed. He has never left me, and under the anointing bears me up, and makes me bold as a lion bearing witness for my Master. Amen.

For a more complete record of my life get my book, "Signs and Wonders."

Oh, the wonders of creation,

And the work of nature's God,

Call forth songs of admiration

As we travel life's rough road.

Chapter 1

The Spirit Reveals the Deep Things of God

THIS IS NOT UNDERSTOOD BY ANY ONE EXCEPT HE HAS THE HOLY GHOST.

Eye hath not seen, nor ear heard, neither have entered into the heart of man, the things which God hath prepared for them that love him. But God hath revealed them unto us by his Spirit: for the Spirit searcheth all things, yea, the deep things of God (1 Corinthians 2:9-10).

Many today apply this to eternity, to the other world; they think we never know these things until we get into another world. I am glad the scripture explains itself. "Eye hath not seen," in the natural state. God hath—in the present—revealed unto us by His Spirit. How? By His Spirit in this world. "The Spirit searcheth all things; yea, the deep things of God."

I desire to call your attention, especially, to the fourteenth verse [of 1 Corinthians 2]. "The natural man receiveth not the things of the Spirit of God: for they are foolishness unto him: neither can he know them, because they are spiritually discerned."

The natural man cannot understand this wonderful scripture. There are two classes of men: the spiritual man and the natural man. The natural man is in the "gall of bitterness"; the spiritual man is born of God and walks in the Spirit; he gets out into the deep. The natural man can never discern spiritual things, never hear and understand the work of the Lord; these things pass all human understanding. The wisdom of this world, intellect and science, can never understand the spiritual things of God.

There are two kinds of wisdom; the wisdom of this world is foolishness with God. The wisdom from above, the natural man cannot comprehend; it never enters his imagination to think of the things God hath prepared for those who love Him.

He hath prepared already, and He hath revealed them to us by His Spirit. His Spirit lets us down into the deep things, even the deep things of God. This is what we preach, what we practice, and what we stand on. The work of the Spirit is foolishness to the natural man; but he that hath the Spirit can discern spiritual things.

Various Kinds of Spirits

There are many kinds of power, and many spirits going out in the world today; and we are told to try the spirits; they are many. Everything is revealed by God through the blessed Holy Ghost. There is only one Spirit we want anything to do with; not our own spirit, nor any other spirit, but the Spirit of the living God. As many as are led by the Spirit of God, they are the sons of God; and He will lead us into all truth, all the way; will lead us where we can get the truth. The child of God will be led into the Baptism of the Holy Ghost and fire; the Pentecostal Baptism.

Then we can go from one deep thing to another. The Holy Ghost is sent to us by Jesus Christ, and all gifts come through the Holy Ghost. Jesus said He shall not speak of Himself, but of Me; He will speak to you and show you the things to come. We believe it. Glory to God!

This is the Holy Ghost who came at Pentecost, and turned Jerusalem upside down; and Jesus said that when the Holy Ghost came, He should abide with us forever, even unto the end. The work of the Spirit is foolishness to the natural man; he cannot comprehend it.

Unless you will hear the voice of God, the voice of the natural man will make you attribute what you see, to excitement, or to some other power. When the Holy Ghost is poured out there are always two classes—one is convinced and convicted, and accepts it; the other says, if I accept, I will have to lead a different life, and be a gazing stock for the world. They are not willing to pay the price, so they begin to draw back. First they wonder at the strange acts, then when they won't accept, they begin to despise. Every one who continues to despise the works of the Holy Ghost will perish.

Satanic Power

There are many powers in the world that are not of God, but are counterfeit; but where there is a counterfeit there is always a genuine. No one ever tries to counterfeit anything that is not genuine; that is a sure evidence that it is genuine.

The devil shows his power in a good many ways to deceive people. He tries to substitute some other power for the power of God. It was so in the time of Moses and the time of the prophets. God's power was especially in the world at certain times, and then magicians would come up with their power and show something that seemed similar. One was God; the other was the devil.

Moses went to Egypt to lead the people out. Before Pharaoh he threw down his rod and it became a live serpent. The magicians said they had the same power, so they threw their rods down, and they became serpents. One was of God, and the other was of the devil. Moses did not get scared and run away; he knew God and wouldn't have run if all the serpents in Egypt had come before him.

He stood his ground, and I admire him for it; I do not like a coward. What was the result? Moses' serpent swallowed the others up, head and tail! There was nothing left of them. Those who are trying to overthrow the power of God and substitute something else will have a day of judgment. The time is coming when the Almighty God will manifest His power, then they, too, will be swallowed up.

The Lamb of God left the realms of glory, and came down here to be foot sore, dusty, weary, spit upon; He said, "I am come to do thy will, Oh God." If He had not borne all these things; if He had not gone all the way to the cross, the Holy Ghost never could have come. If He had been left in the tomb, the Holy Ghost never could have come. As soon as He arose from the dead, and ascended into heaven, the Holy Ghost could come.

Christ's Sovereignty

God gave His Son the highest place before all the hosts of heaven; then He sent the Holy Ghost to dwell in these bodies, His temple. The Holy Ghost is a great power; He is compared to wind, water and fire.

At Pentecost He came like a cyclone, a mighty, rushing wind; He is to come like rivers of living water. He comes as fire; tongues of fire sat upon each of them at Pentecost. Wind, water and fire—the most destructive elements we have, yet the most useful.

God uses them to denote the mighty power of the Holy Ghost; and He was to be given after Jesus was glorified. We see many demonstrations of His mighty power, and we can but "speak the things we have seen and heard," of His glory, His majesty. When we know these things, we are witnesses to His power. His majesty and His glory. Glory to God!

He is a mighty power, and He lives in these bodies. He lets down an "eternal weight of glory" upon us here, and when we are filled with this glory we have to give vent to it, sometimes, or we would explode. What are we? Only worms of the dust; we cannot stand the glory of God; one breath from Him lays us prostrate.

In the Bible we read how men fell when they had a glimpse of God's glory. St. Paul tells us there are those who have a form of godliness, but deny the power thereof; from such we are to turn away. "In the last days perilous times shall come," and those who have reprobate minds shall withstand God's children to their faces, even as the magicians withstood Moses.

In the last days there will be some people living very near to God; but the devil will have his workers, too; who will attribute signs and wonders done to any power except the power of Christ. The Lamb of God, the Lion of the tribe of Judah, has never lost His power, and never will lose His power, and I would hate to say by my actions that I thought the devil had more power than God.

God's Power Unlike Any Other

There is a wonderful difference between the power of God and any of those other powers. The Holy Ghost comes only in Christ; He only comes into the bodies of those who love God. When He takes possession of us, He takes us away into the sweetest experience this side of heaven, alone with God. He talks to us and reveals to us "things to come" (John 16:13).

It is wonderful! God puts us under the power, and God takes us out. No man can bestow this power upon another; it comes only through Jesus Christ. There are two kinds of power, and people who do not know the difference will stand up today and say wisdom is foolishness.

Many people today have an intellectual faith, a historical faith; they believe; well, the devils believe and tremble; belief is one thing, faith is another. "The letter killeth; the Spirit giveth life." If the truth is hid, it is hid to those who are lost.

We may have intellectual imaginations, go through a course of study, learning the doctrines of men; yet there is none but the Holy

Ghost who can give us a real abiding, tangible definite knowledge of "the things of God." They seem foolish to the natural man. Sometimes the Holy Ghost gives a Spirit of laughter, and sometimes of weeping, and every one in the place will be affected by the Spirit.

I have stood before thousands of people and could not speak, just weeping. When I was able to see, people were weeping everywhere; that is one way the Holy Ghost works. I have stood an hour with my hand raised, held by the mighty power of God. When I came to myself and saw the people, their faces were shining.

"God moves in mysterious ways His wonders to perform." He is the God I worship. Jesus says, "Here am I and the children Thou hast given me." We believe in "signs and wonders," not from beneath, but from above. We are a people to be wondered at; we are for a sign among the people.

Citizenship

The heaven of heavens cannot contain God, yet He tabernacles with men; He comes and dwells in us. His gifts are demonstrated through us, that people may know God dwells in Zion; we have a bodyguard of angels. The angels of the Lord encamp around those who love God. "Our citizenship is in heaven," and we are on the way.

The Holy Ghost works in many ways. People saw the fire on the disciples' heads at Pentecost; they staggered like drunken men; then the Holy Ghost took possession of their tongues. God Almighty spoke through 120 of His children, and they were telling of His wonderful works. They did not know what they were saying, but every man heard them speak in his own tongue wherein he was born.

I am glad God does the same thing today. People who are not saved hate the power of God; the cold, dead, formalists cannot understand the power of God; it is foolishness to them; they think people are excited, hypnotized, have lost their mind.

May God have mercy upon us if we do not know God's power from hypnotic power, or devil power! If any man speak against the Holy Ghost it shall never be forgiven him; to attribute the work of the Holy Ghost to the devil, or to any unclean spirit cannot be forgiven; that is the unpardonable sin.

Some people are calling the Holy Ghost the devil, and they had better beware. There are different kinds of spirits, and different kinds of power; and the natural man cannot understand the work of the Holy Spirit— shining faces, singing, shouting, as one, to make one sound (2 Chronicles 5:13); sometimes staggering and falling, "drunken, but not with wine"; sometimes speaking with "other tongues."

Spiritual Manifestation in Angelic Singing

Praise God, some of the redeemed are getting so filled with the Holy Ghost that He is singing through them songs that none but the redeemed can sing, "there are diversities of operations, but the same Spirit" (1 Corinthians 12:4,6, author's paraphrase). Paul tells us, the Spirit will work in you in one way, and in some one else in another way; you know it is the same Spirit, and you do not get jealous because the other is blessed; no matter how the Spirit works, every member of the body is profited.

People look on these things; they see us lift up holy hands to God; and they don't like it; they are too dead, they could not get their hands up. Paul says, "I will...that men pray every where, lifting up holy hands" (1 Timothy 2:8). The Psalmist says, "O clap your hands, all ye people; shout unto God with the voice of triumph" (Psalm 47:1).

People go to the theatre and clap their hands; but when we get our grave clothes off and begin to clap our hands, they think it an awful thing. David danced with all his might before the ark; and sometimes the Spirit of God gets into our feet, and makes them like "hinds' feet."

David says, "By my God have I leaped over a wall" (Psalm 18:29). How much more in these last days when we are getting ready for a flight in the air! We must get a good supply of this power; the same power that took Jesus up will take us up one day.

We want more of it, don't we? More of this mighty power. No matter what people say, foolishness, hypnotism, and every other thing; that doesn't make it so. The Spirit will take us out into the deep things, even "the deep things of God."

Old Testament Types Revealed
Through the Spirit in the New

Many things recorded in the Old Testament are types of the work of the Spirit in the New. Many of the movements of God through His children seemed foolishness, and the messages He gave His prophets to carry, humanly speaking, seemed very foolish.

He gave Noah a plan of the ark; only one window, only one door. He built it according to God's plan, not heeding the jeers of the people, who thought he was losing his mind. He was a gazing stock for everybody, but he went on with the building, and proved the wisdom of God in the end.

He built the ark, and God provided the water, more water than they wanted; too much water for them. What happened? God took those who believed Him into the ark and shut the door. The water rose and the ark went above the tree-tops—as we are going some day. God is building the ark now; and the works of the Holy Ghost are foolishness to the people who are fighting them.

The ark sailed away and the world went down, all except Noah and his family. Not many are going into the ark God is building; people are crying, "foolishness." One time there was a great battle; the enemy had gathered like grasshoppers. God knew there were a lot of cowards among his people, and He tested them until only three hundred were left to meet the enemy.

The Leader-The Signal-The Results

God can work by the few as well as the many. He told Gideon what to do; He divided the men into three companies and, "put a trumpet in every man's hand, with empty pitchers, and lamps within the pitchers" (Judges 7:16). He said, "When I give the signal, blow the trumpet and say, 'The sword of the Lord and of Gideon'" (v. 18 paraphrase).

As they obeyed their leader, something happened—God always has a leader. At the signal, they blew the trumpets, broke the pitchers, revealing the lamps; and they shouted, "The Sword of the Lord and of Gideon."

At the shout and the light the enemy was frightened to death, and started to run; but God sent confusion among them. That little band of three hundred "cranks" put the whole host of the enemy to flight. What they did seemed foolish, did it not? But what was the outcome? The whole army of the enemy was conquered.

God used a vision—He does sometimes. He let Gideon go down to the enemy's camp and he heard a man tell his fellows a vision or dream, how a "cake of barley bread tumbled into the host of Midian, and came unto a tent, and smote it that it fell, and overturned it, that the tent lay along" (Judges 7:13).

The other interpreted it, "This is nothing else save the sword of Gideon ... into his hand hath God delivered Midian, and all the host" (Judges 7:14). So Gideon believed and took courage.

Children of God, who think you are something, you are nothing; when you realize you are nothing, God fights for you. How foolish seemed the method of fighting the Midianites! Israel might have said, if we break the pitchers, the lamps will show the enemy where we are and they will shoot us. When God speaks go forward, obey Him; He takes care of His own.

Truly, God moves in a mysterious way. Remember the fall of Jericho. It had great walls around it, and all the people were shut in. God said to Joshua that he and his men of war should march around the city once a day for six days, [with] seven priests bearing before the ark seven trumpets of rams' horns; on the seventh day they were to march around the city seven times, the priests blowing with the trumpets; and when they made a long blast the people were to shout, and the walls should fall down.

It took faith to do all that marching without any sign of victory, to shout, anyone can shout after the walls fall. Humanly speaking, how foolish this all was, don't you see? No preparation for war, only marching, and blowing rams' horns; but that was God's way and they were simple enough to obey God! What was the result? The walls went down.

So we could go all through the Word of God; so many things that seem so silly, things people would laugh at, but it was God's way, and His servants were willing to obey Him. The result showed the wonderful wisdom and brought victory through a visible display of His power.

Apparent Ignorance in the Natural Is Height Upon Height in Wisdom in the Spiritual

When these visible signs came, they put a fear of God upon the people; it is so with the works of the Holy Ghost. The ways of God are foolishness to the natural man, and the works of the Spirit are foolishness to the natural man; but what is the outcome?

Paul said, "If any man among you seemeth to be wise in this world, let him become a fool, that he may be wise" (1 Corinthians 3:18). Later he said, "I will come to visions and revelations of the Lord" (2 Corinthians 12:1). He said he was carried away to the third heaven—whether in the body or out of the body, he could not tell—he could not tell whether his whole body went or not; he was so light he could not tell whether he had left his body here or not.

He said, "God knoweth"; and he heard unutterable things. At another time Paul was praying in the temple and fell under the power of God; he fell into a trance; he appeared to be unconscious to the world, but he was never so wide awake to God in his life.

It is then the Spirit of God lets us down into the deep things, even the deep things of God. Peter fell into a trance upon the housetop and God spoke to him three times. Paul and Silas started out to visit converts. Paul had a vision; he saw a man of Macedonia holding out his hands and saying, "Come over and help us." He knew it was the call of God, so they changed their course and went to this place, altogether different from their plans.

When they began to preach and were arrested, they might have thought they had been mistaken, but Paul knew God, and he never doubted it was God's voice that had called him. They might have said, if we had not come here we would have had many people to preach to; now we have come to this strange place, [and] have been put in prison, with our feet fast in the stocks. The devil put them in there, but God permitted it, and God delivered them.

There are many wonderful things all about us in these last days, things the natural man cannot understand; demonstration of God's power. There are other powers, too, and many do not know the difference. God's power is the greatest, and is the only power that will bring peace to your soul.

God wants you to be pure and holy, filled with the Holy Ghost; but the devil is right here, too, and if you do not know the difference you will be listening to him. He comes sometimes as an angel of light. One word in the Garden of Eden upset the world; the little word "not".

When God talks to you, the message agrees with the written Word; the Holy Ghost never says anything that doesn't correspond with the Word. A message that comes from heaven must correspond with the word; if otherwise, do not accept it.

The things of the Spirit that seem foolishness to the world antagonize the devil; and he sometimes does things that look very similar, but to him who understands, there is a wonderful difference. I have been carried away in the Spirit many, many times.

Once I was seven hours under the power of God. I have been examined at such a time by medical doctors and found to be in a normal condition. Many I know of have been honest enough to say the power was not hypnotic, even while they could not understand it.

Celebrated Hypnotist Baffled

One of the greatest hypnotists in the world came to our meeting in St. Louis; he had been there two or three days before I knew anything about it. He was surprised to see a man lying there whom hundreds of hypnotists had tried to get under their power; he himself had tried it.

He went to him and tried to bring him out, but could not. After a while the hypnotist came to me to have an interview with me; he said he was going to call his friends together and tell them he had found something he could not understand.

He said, "If there is a God, I believe this is His power." He could not put any one under that power, nor bring any one out. When the doctors examined me when I was lying under the power, they said my pulse was regular, my blood flowing naturally, my heart in a natural condition.

I am told that when a person is hypnotized, the blood does not flow naturally, the person is unconscious, and simply does what he is told; some one has to put him in that state, and bring him out again.

God does lay His people down under His power, and then He talks to them. I have known people to be a whole week under the power of God. May He seal these truths to our hearts!

I know nothing about hypnotic power; I never saw a person hypnotized; but I do know something of the power of God, of the power of the Holy Ghost. It is God Himself who sends this power; we can press the button, but God sends the power.

Talk about excitement! This power is the best thing in the world to settle the nerves. These people go down praising God, while they are there, and when they are up they are still giving God praise.

"Let every thing that hath breath praise the Lord" (Psalm 150:6). People ask why we tell them to praise the Lord. If you do not feel it at first, praise as a "sacrifice," and after a while the praise will come of itself, from a soul filled with joy. Hallelujah!

If you will search your Bible you will find the things I have told you are true. My words do not amount to anything unless they are backed up by God's Word. The Lord gave me this message tonight and I have written it to you.

When the power of the Spirit has been so maligned, it is time for you to take a stand for the truth. When a ship is in danger, the sailors come to the front, if they are not cowards. Let us come to the front, not run away.

I stand here in defense of the Gospel. If we are faithful, all things must work together for God's glory. Praise His Name.

Chapter 2

"Try the Spirits"

Beloved,...try the spirits (1 John 4:1).

THERE ARE MANY SPIRITS WE DO NOT WANT TO HAVE ANYTHING to do with. There is our own spirit; the flesh and the devil. There are many spirits contending, and many times we let our own spirit rule and make ourselves think it is God; the same, with the flesh and the devil.

Sometimes we know it is not God, but we want to have our own way. If we have the Holy Ghost we can prove the spirits, because everything the Holy Ghost does is confirmed by The Word. We do not want to trust to tongues and interpretations, you must measure things by The Word; we must measure tongues and demonstrations by The Word, and if they do not agree with The Word, we must not accept them; everything must be measured by The Word.

We do know God and the voice of God, but the devil can come as an angel of light. When you are in the Holy Ghost, that is the time the devil tries to get in and lead you astray. The Holy Ghost is revealing some secret things; at the same time the devil comes in, and if you are not careful, you will listen to what he has to say and follow him.

Once I was having a wonderful vision, and right in the midst of it the devil said to me, "You are going to die." I was very poorly and was worked nearly to death and I listened to the devil for a minute; then I stopped to hear what God wanted to teach me.

I said, "What is this God is showing me? Does this agree with what God is showing?" I saw there was a big difference. God touched my forehead, the seat of intellect and reason; [and] my mouth, signifying courage and power to give forth the message; and I could not die if I was to do this; if I was to give the people His message, I was not going to die.

There was someone in the meeting here God was blessing. He wanted to use her, but the devil came in and made her think she could do any kind of outrageous thing and it would be of God.

See how the devil can lead us off. She was talking in tongues and praying, and she said, "Lord, if you want me to kill anyone, I will do it; if you want me to set the camp on fire, I will do it."

Holy Ghost and the Word

That is the way in spiritualism; the Holy Ghost never does anything like that; He does not come to kill and knock people's heads off; He deals with them in love and tenderness. People have even offered up children in sacrifice. If you listen to God, the devil will be put to one side.

These things hurt the Pentecostal Movement; God is in it, but the devil is in it, too. Many people are honest, but they do not understand. God shows great things that are going to happen and the devil comes in and makes them set a date.

Daniel did not understand the vision he had for some time. An angel appeared to him to make him understand the vision. Be careful the devil does not come in and give you another meaning all together different from what God wants you to have.

So many prophesy this or that, and it never comes true; the prophecy was not according to the Word of God. Some one gives a person a message and he believes God sent it, when it is not according to the Word.

When God calls you out for His work He will take care of you, give you something to eat and clothe you; there are so many who run before they are sent; better not [to] go at all. Sometimes the devil uses tongues to upset things generally; the devil can speak in tongues, and your flesh can.

When God speaks in tongues, it means something, and you want to look for interpretation. God says ask for interpretation. Sometimes God gives it through someone else, but give the person who speaks in tongues a chance to interpret. Be careful you do not give an interpretation in your own spirit; this hurts the work everywhere. Let us try the spirits and not get in the flesh.

Some people, if they do not like anyone, will give a message in tongues, or a rebuke and nearly knock the person's head off. This is the work of the devil. Then someone will get up—some people are so silly—and say,"Don't lay hands on that; it is the Holy Ghost"; and no one dares to touch it, and the devil has the whole thing.

It goes out that the leader sanctions all that, and people do not want to have anything to do with it. The leader may have discernment, but some one will pull his coat-tail and say,"Don't lay hands on that." Instead of being so afraid, let us search the Scriptures. God never told anyone to rebuke in an ugly tone.

There was a great work being done in the West. One woman, especially, said the United States was going to be destroyed, and they should go to Japan. They went. People who could not spare the money helped them; they went to escape the wreck.

The whole thing was of the devil. The United States were not destroyed; they could not speak the Japanese language; they were stranded and a number backslid; they tried to raise money for a great building, but never accomplished it. They had been doing a good work here, but other spirits got in.

God gave me a special commission to take the precious from the vile; and I do not want you to get into the snare of the devil. So many young people, after their baptism, give up work and go to preaching. In a few days they tell all they know, then tell something they don't know; bread and butter does not come in, and many of them backslide.

If God doesn't send you out, don't give up your work; then you will have something to give. This mistake is made by many missionaries who go abroad; some sell all they have, break up their homes, separate from their wives, and God has not called them.

Gifts and Requirements

The Holy Ghost makes us level-headed. Those who stayed in the camp got as much as they who went. Be God's stewards and give the Lord His part. The cattle upon a thousand hills are His, but He works through our instrumentality. He gives you everything you have, physical, financial and spiritual; and He expects you to use all your powers for Him; if you give out, He will supply.

He expects you to take Him into partnership, and give Him what belongs to Him; and He will bless you. The Gospel has to be supported. Water is free, but it costs money to lay the pipes and keep the water running. Angels can fly, but men have to pay [transportation] fare and someone has to help.

If you keep the pipes in order, the Gospel will be given out, and you need to help with your prayers, hold up the hands of those who work. If you trust God and walk with Him, that is the work God wants of you.

Don't take up with every vision that comes along. In the Pentecostal Movement, in some places, they have discarded the Word of God. They don't want a leader, and God always had a leader; when there is none, the devil takes the chair. God hath set some pastors and teachers (Ephesians 4:11).

How does any one know when God calls them to the ministry? Some one has said that when God calls anyone to do His work, you can hardly get him into the pulpit; but when the devil calls him, you can't keep him out of it.

Some people want to talk so much, bringing in a bone of contention; and it is hurting the work everywhere. Leave outside issues. God will teach people what to eat, what to wear, and where to go. Many of God's children are nagging about these things. The Lord said, if you do not think it right to eat meat, don't do it; but don't judge another.

When we open our mouths, let us say something. If you have the baptism, you need not tell it; people will know it. Let God speak to you; do not wait for someone to speak in tongues and tell you God wants you to go to India; let God speak to you.

People who go because someone else says so get homesick and discouraged and try to get back again. Let the Lord be our guide; if we do His will, we shall know His will.

Hold up Jesus and try to get the people so full of the Holy Ghost that they will live in unity. We do not want to lay hands on anyone suddenly. If we do anything in a spirit of contention, the first thing we know everything is in a jumble, and we have done more harm in one meeting than can be imagined.

Hold up Jesus and the Resurrection. Let us walk in the light, as He is in the light. Christ is the great Headlight and I am on the stretch for more light than I ever saw in my life; you have fellowship when you walk in the light. We are the lower lights and He will show us what to do next.

He will say to you, now you can do this; you may say, I did not know before that you would trust me; and again His answer, you can do it now.

Until God shows you a thing it is not a sin, but after He shows it to you, if you do it, it is a sin. Consecrate everything to God, day by day. He will not call you to do a thing unless He is going to give you strength and grace.

Having a Teachable Spirit

When you go into a meeting, listen to the teaching; if it does not suit you and you want something else, the best thing you can do is to go out quietly and drum up a crowd yourself. Some say you have no need that any man should teach you; the natural man cannot teach you, but the spiritual man can teach you.

We know what we are talking about; the spiritual man can teach you. We know nothing as we should, and there is so much for us to know.

Be careful not to lay hands suddenly on anyone. Regarding the recent disturbance here, we profess to be saints and we want to show forth the Spirit of Christ. We must be firm, but kind. Do not speak roughly. The crowd want to see. I would have nearly broken my neck when I was young to see what you are seeing.

When they became noisy, it would have been useless to attempt to use force; it would only have ended in a fight, and the plan of the enemy would have been accomplished. God led me in the only way by which the disturbance could be quelled, and order restored; God fought for us. Do not speak roughly to the boys; each one is some mother's boy. God can smite with conviction; the battle is His, not ours.

"Try the spirits." In one of our meetings there was a colored woman* who had wonderful experience spiritually; that is the kind the devil gets after. One day she commenced to go about on her knees, twisting about like a serpent. God does not tell anyone to do that. She spoke in tongues; then she said, "I don't want to do it; I don't want to do it."

Everyone knew it was not of God; and I said to her, "that is not God; the enemy has got hold of you." At first she didn't want to give up, but the next day God showed her and she asked to be delivered. The devil had got in and made her do things that were not right, to kill her influence.

Spiritualistic and Spiritualism—the Difference

A woman came to me and said, "I am afraid this spirit on me is not of God; I was baptized in the Holy Ghost; I went into a mission where they did everything by tongues and they got me so mixed up I did not know where I was; then this spirit got hold of me; it shakes my head and makes my head ache."

That is spiritualism. Some people, when they pray for anyone and lay on hands, throw their slime off. That is spiritualism. Don't ever do anything like that. When you lay hands on a person, God takes care of the evil spirit. If you are filled with the Holy Ghost, the devil is outside you; keep him out. Be careful who lays hands on you, for the devil is counterfeiting God's work.

For two years that woman could not give a testimony. God rebuked the shaking spirit, the power of God came in her hands and in her voice, and she gave a testimony for God.

That is what ails the Pentecostal Movement; so much of this has crept in. Some people take every foolish thing for the Holy Ghost. There are two extremes; one keeps the Holy Ghost from working, except in a certain channel; and the other thinks everything is of the Holy Ghost; "don't lay hands on it." One is as bad as the other. Let everything be done by the Word of God.

We are living in the last days and there has got to be a higher standard for the Pentecostal Movement. Christ is coming, and we cannot move along in the old rut. God is sifting us today and we have got to rise above errors; we have to rise up and go forward. By the grace of God we will. Praise His Name!

---

*Editor's Note: The terms used to refer to different races considered acceptable in Mrs. Woodworth-Etter's day are offensive and unacceptable today. Inclusion of these terms does not in any way reflect the attitude or policies of Harrison House.

Chapter 3

The Unpardonable Sin

IN THE STONE CHURCH, CHICAGO, ILLINOIS, JULY 6, 1913.

Dear Friends: We have met in the presence of the most high God; we have come to do business for Jehovah. Let us do it well. We shall meet again in eternity. Let us be very solemn. God's reporter is taking note of every thought, every action here tonight, of those who are against Him and those who are for Him. So let us turn our minds from the fleetings of life, the things that are passing away, and be shut in with God this hour.

The message the Lord has brought before us tonight will be found in the 12th chapter of Matthew, verses 31 and 32.

> Wherefore I say unto you, All manner of sin and blasphemy shall be forgiven unto men: but the blasphemy against the Holy Ghost shall not be forgiven unto men. And whosoever speaketh a word against the Son of man, it shall be forgiven him: but whosoever speaketh against the Holy Ghost, it shall not be forgiven him, neither in this world, neither in the world to come.

This message comes to us from Jesus tonight as much as if He was standing here. Hear the eternal word from the lips of the Son of God now reigning in glory. The words are just as powerful as when they fell from His lips, if they go out by the power of the Holy Ghost. This subject is considered one of the deepest in the Word of God. You have often heard the question asked, "What is the unpardonable sin?" And some people are very much concerned about having committed it. John says: "There is a sin unto death. I do not say that you shall pray for it," but other sins are not unto death, and through prayer God will wash them all out.

The Danger of Blasphemy

Blasphemy against God and all kinds of sin against Him and against mankind will be blotted out, but whosoever speaks against the Holy Ghost hath no forgiveness neither in this world nor in the world to come. Christ said this because they said He had an evil spirit and did His mighty works through that agency. So, you see, it is an unpardonable sin to attribute any of the mighty works of the Holy Ghost to the devil. There has never been a time since the early church when there was so much danger of people committing the unpardonable sin as there is today since the Pentecostal fire has girdled the earth and tens of thousands have received the Holy Ghost, feeling His presence, backed up by signs and wonders and divers operations of the Spirit.

When men and women come in contact with this work of the Holy Ghost, hearing His words and seeing His works, there is danger lest they attribute the power present to some other agency other than the Spirit of God. There is danger lest they condemn the power and condemn God's servants. How often have we heard ministers say, when they heard men and women and children speaking in other tongues, "Oh, it is the work of the devil." Now you hear what God says about it; they are speaking against the Holy Ghost. God has been working in this city and is going to work in much greater measure. We expect to see greater signs and wonders; if the saints stand together as one, pray together and shout victory, God will show Himself a mighty God and a Savior.

He Comes in Many Ways

He will not only come in healing power, but will manifest Himself in many mighty ways. On the Day of Pentecost, Peter said, "God hath poured forth this which ye see and hear." And from what they heard and saw three thousand owned [acknowledged] it was the power of God and turned to Christ. Others stifled conviction, and turned away saying, "This is the work of the devil." When the Holy Ghost is poured out it is either life unto life or death unto death. It is life unto life to those who go forward and death unto death to those who blaspheme against the Holy Ghost. So we want to be careful what we say against the divers operations, supernatural signs and workings of the Holy Ghost. Some people look on and say, "It looks like hypnotism," "I believe it is mesmerism." To others it appears mere foolishness, even as Scripture says of the natural man, "The things of the Spirit of God are foolishness unto him and he cannot know them because they are spiritually discerned" (1 Corinthians 2:14, author's paraphrase).

It was the same on the Day of Pentecost, when a multitude saw the disciples staggering about under the power of the Spirit, speaking in tongues. While some said, "They are drunken," others knew the mighty power of God was there. There is a power here that is not of earth, a power lifting people up, making men and women upright, making them good neighbors, good husbands and wives. It is the mighty power and presence of the Almighty God. Watch the lives of these people; they do not seek worldly amusements, but the power of God is manifested in them. What did the power bring on the Day of Pentecost? The crowd that came together were all amazed and said, "We never saw it on this fashion." Everybody began to get convicted; though some, not willing to accept it, not willing to be called fools for Christ's sake, rejected it and to ease their guilty consciences, said, "They are drunken." They knew better. They knew the mighty power of God was there and if there was a question God settled it. Peter got up in the midst of the brethren and said: "These are not drunken, as you say. Men don't get drunk at nine o'clock in the morning; but this is that which was spoken by Joel the prophet: 'In the last days I will pour out my Spirit upon all flesh. Your young men shall see visions, your old men shall dream dreams.' This is the Holy Ghost which you now see and hear" (Acts 2:15-18, author's paraphrase). It is the same Holy Ghost tonight. The Holy Ghost is the Spirit of God. He is a person and works under the directions of Jesus Christ, under His orders. He doesn't do anything but what Christ tells him to do. When we are ready to receive Him, Jesus sends the Holy Ghost to impart to us His own gifts. The Holy Ghost cleanses these temples and comes in to dwell. He fills these bodies and His power in us gives us utterance in tongues and works through us in many other ways. Now, in order to guard against committing the unpardonable sin, we must know a little of who the Holy Ghost is. He could not come until Christ was glorified. Christ was on the earth in His human body for only a short time, but at Pentecost He came through the Holy Ghost to stay.

The Mission of the Holy Ghost

Jesus said that when the Holy Ghost should come whom the Father would send in His Name, "He shall abide with you forever." And He will not speak of Himself, but what He hears He will say. Oh, I love the Holy Ghost because He is always witnessing for Jesus and He comes to bring us power. He is "the Comforter, the Spirit of truth," who shall "abide forever." He brings all things to our remembrance. We are so forgetful in our natural state; but we have a spiritual mind and God writes His word in our minds and on the tablets of our hearts and the Holy Spirit brings these messages to us at the right time—a message to this one in sin, that one in sorrow, encouraging the weak and helping the strong with some message from heaven, always pointing us to Jesus the great Burden-Bearer—rivers of living water flowing from the individual, healing virtue going out.

Virtue went out from Peter so that the sick were healed upon whom his mere shadow fell. Power went out from Paul so that they sent handkerchiefs and aprons from his body and through them, when they were laid on the afflicted, streams of healing went forth and devils were driven out. The Holy Ghost is called "Water." "I will pour water upon him that is thirsty, and floods upon the dry ground" (Isaiah 44:3). A tidal wave of glory is coming this way. God help us to be as empty vessels that the Holy Ghost's power may fill us to overflowing. The Holy Ghost is spoken of as "fire," "wind" and "water"—three of the most destructive elements in the world and three of the most useful.

Mighty Winds and Heavenly Zephyrs

We could not live without fire, wind or water. When a cyclone comes men and women turn pale. When God's cyclone through the Holy Ghost strikes the people it is a great leveler. They lose sight of their money bags and all hatred and ill-will are swept away as a cyclone carries all before it. When a tidal wave strikes a city it submerges everything; so, in a tidal wave of the Holy Ghost, everything goes under. Oh, we want a cyclone of God's power to sweep out of our lives everything that cumbers us, and a tidal wave to submerge us in God.

God uses these great elements, fire, wind and water, in all their force to give us an idea of the mighty power of the Holy Ghost. Our bodies are His temples and, as great pieces of mechanism are moved by electricity, so our bodies, the most wonderful piece of mechanism ever known, are moved by the power of the Holy Ghost sent down from heaven. He filled the one hundred and twenty on the Day of Pentecost with power to witness for Jesus. At the hands of the apostles, God healed the sick and He heals today by the same power that was on the apostles. God pours out rivers of living waters. What manner of people ought we to be?

If we haven't the power, let us confess it and ask God to give us the power He gave the first disciples. If those who come to the Lord will be filled as they were on the Day of Pentecost, we will have streams of living water rushing through us and flowing to the very ends of the earth. Jesus Christ was baptized in the Holy Ghost, but He did not have all power until He had finished His course. He could have turned away and not have gone to the cross, but He went all the way and cried, "It is finished." His last act was this going down into death.

But God Almighty raised Him up and when He came up all power was given Him—ALL POWER! He sent His disciples out in His Name and said that those who believed on Him should cast out devils, should speak in new tongues, should lay hands on the sick, and if they drank any deadly things (accidentally, of course) it would not hurt them. He said to the disciples, "Do not marvel at what you see. These things shall ye do if ye believe, and greater works than these shall ye do because I go to the Father" (John 14:12, author's paraphrase).

The Pentecost Shower Falls

Now when Pentecost came they were all in the upper room waiting. They were all saved and all pure and of one accord—no divisions, no controversy. They did not know how the "promise of the Father" was going to come, but they were waiting for it; and suddenly the Spirit, as a cyclone, came and filled the whole building; a great tidal wave of power was turned upon them and they were all filled with living water.

The Spirit's tongues of fire were upon their heads and they all began to speak in other tongues as the Holy Ghost gave them utterance. The people who came running up were amazed and said, "What does this mean? Are not all these that speak Galileans? Are they not ignorant of these foreign tongues? Yet everyone hears them speak in his own language wherein he was born. It was the Holy Ghost who gave them utterance in languages. The Lord had said, "With men of other lips and stammering tongues will I speak unto this people, but for all that they will not believe." [1]

He put the stress on that and the people heard and knew, yet for all this they mocked and cried out that the men had been drinking. The Holy Ghost came to testify of Jesus. The Spirit preached the first sermon on Jesus' resurrection through Peter, who got up and brought forward the Scripture to prove that this manifestation was of the Holy Ghost, and that He witnessed to Christ.

Peter Preaches First Pentecostal Sermon

People who had not believed that Jesus was the Christ—though He did works that none other did and spake as never man spake—were now brought under conviction and three thousand souls were converted on that day. Many in Jerusalem, when they saw the operations of the Holy Ghost, believed, and "a great company of the priests were obedient to the faith" (Acts 6:7).

The Holy Ghost is here tonight bringing Jesus into our midst. He is healing the sick by the power of God today, devils are being cast out, and miracles are being wrought in the mighty Name of Jesus through the power of the Holy Ghost. God is giving visions. The prophet says, "Where there is no vision, the people perish" (Proverbs 29:18). People are having visions today of the second coming of the Lord, visions of the marriage supper of the Lamb and of the Rapture. The Holy Ghost comes with weeping. He makes you weep because of what is coming on the earth. Oh, there is a sign of trouble! The unbelieving world is going to be cast out into darkness; but while we sigh and weep at the sad condition of the world, we rejoice to know that Jesus is coming soon.

Prophecy Comes True

We were holding meetings in Moline. One night an evangelist came in whom we had never seen before. We were talking about the Baptism of the Holy Ghost, which she had heard about and was hungry for. I said to her, "You are going to get the Baptism tonight." There was not much sign of it as I got up to give the word. She sat in front of me and while I was talking she looked as if she was asleep, but the power of God was upon her. The Word was going out and the lightning struck. When I got through talking the power was on her in a wonderful way and she commenced speaking in tongues and interpreting.

Then she would wail the most sad wail I ever heard; it struck me it was like the daughters of Jerusalem weeping over the destruction of the temple; so painful, so doleful was it, everyone was made sad. I said, "This is the signal of some great sorrow, great distress, great anguish and trouble that is coming on the people." God showed me it was a signal of distress, of awful calamity that was coming. At the same time a sister said that she saw a great earthquake, and described how the water swept over the corpses and down the street. The next day there came out in the papers an account of the dreadful destruction by earthquake at Kingston, Jamaica.

Do you not see the hand of God in that vision? It was something that, coming true immediately, would convince the people. In Dallas last year the Lord showed us many things that took place in Turkey when the armies came together. An old brother in Dallas had visions of the battles before they took place and saw multitudes being killed.

One night there was a loud report as of a terrible explosion. About sixty of the saints heard it and the congregation felt the shock. As soon as the news could reach us we heard about it through the papers. The Holy Ghost brings gifts, miracles, discerning of spirits. We laugh and cry in the Spirit, we shout and dance and leap; our bodies get so light we scarcely touch the earth.

The Spirit Gives Heavenly Music

At our last meeting at Long Hill, Connecticut, the heavenly choir surpassed anything I had ever heard. We had it two or three times a day, and there wasn't a discord. It was the Holy Ghost making harmony through these bodies and the singing was no earthly singing, but heavenly. Sometimes I would be a little late in getting to the meeting and as I came up the hill the sound of the heavenly choir was wafted down. It sounded as if it came from heaven; it was the song of the redeemed.

Song That Only the Redeemed Can Sing

God is getting His children ready to sing at the marriage supper of the Lamb. They sing a song no one can sing except the redeemed. No outsiders can join them. The Spirit has shown me the coming of the Lord is very near and I know it now more than ever. God baptized me over twenty-five years ago with a wonderful baptism, but I am more hungry today than I ever was. I see greater possibilities today than ever before. Let us go on from one degree to another. Blessed is the servant who, when His master comes, is found at His post, giving to the household their portion of meat in due season. This is your opportunity, your day of God's visitation. "The bride hath made herself ready." You can not go to the tailor and order your suit to go to the banquet; you have to make it yourself. The bride hath made herself ready and it is going to be the most wonderful wedding garment you ever heard of.

It takes skill to weave the garment of pure linen and embroider the "fine wrought linen work" and when she is ready He will greatly admire her. There will be a great company of guests in the banquet hall. But some of us are not ready; we haven't our garments. The time has come to get ready. Oh, it means something to dress for the marriage supper of the Lamb. When there is a banquet in honor of the King's son or daughter, it is a great occasion and the musicians are trained for it long before. Now this banquet that is going to take place in the skies, this marriage supper, of the Lamb, will be the greatest wedding that was ever known.

The King's Bride

The King of Glory will be married to His bride. Don't you know that every good thing the world enjoys God is going to let us enjoy ten thousand fold? That will be the greatest banquet, the most wonderful occasion ever heard of, when we shall eat bread and drink wine in the kingdom. The bride is now in training, the Holy Ghost is the Dove; the singing is the cooing of the dove before the storm. Did you ever hear the doves before the storm calling to their mates to seek shelter? So the Holy Ghost is cooing and chirping, calling us to seek shelter from the tribulation storms that are coming upon the earth. The Lord is having us in training, making our bodies light and supple so that we can go up. May the Lord help us to be filled with the Holy Ghost so that we can rise. It is the only moving power in the Church of Christ, the mighty agent. He was sent to carry on business through His Body. Let us get the fire from heaven that will enable us to do business for God, and be careful that we do not attribute the power of God to the devil lest we commit the unpardonable sin.

Chapter 4

Christ's Great
Revival on the Plains

AND IT CAME TO PASS IN THOSE DAYS, THAT HE WENT OUT into a mountain to pray, and continued all night in prayer to God.

And when it was day, he called unto him his disciples: and of them he chose twelve, whom also he named apostles....

And he came down with them, and stood in the plain, and the company of his disciples, and a great multitude of people out of all Judaea and Jerusalem, and from the sea coast of Tyre and Sidon, which came to hear him, and to be healed of their diseases;

And they that were vexed with unclean spirits: and they were healed.

And the whole multitude sought to touch him, for there went virtue out of him, and healed them all (Luke 6:12-13, 17-19).

This is one of the greatest revivals that Jesus Christ ever held with great and wonderful results. We find much preceding these verses, where the Son of God had healed a lame man who had a withered arm, the time the devil got up in the people and they tried to kill the Son of God, but He slipped away from the crowd and went into the mountains and prayed all night alone with God. If the Son of God found it necessary to pray all night alone with God, don't you think we ought to spend some time alone with God? He was probably fasting. When Jesus Christ fasted something happened afterwards, and if God puts a fast upon you and you go in God's way something will happen afterwards besides afflicting your body and being all out of sorts when you are through and making everybody miserable around you. That is not God's fast. Always when Jesus went out and fasted and prayed some great miracle took place afterwards. When Jesus got His baptism at the Jordan the Holy Ghost came upon Him to stay and He was led away into the wilderness where He was alone with God forty days, fasting all that time. After the forty days the fast was over and He was hungry, but He was not hungry all the time He was fasting, but afterwards, we are told, He was hungry. The devil is always at hand, so the devil tempted Him in a wonderful way by asking Him to make bread out of stones. Of course He could have done it, but you see He got power while fasting with God and communing with the Spirit, to meet the devil. He [the devil] came with all his satanic force against Son of God. But He [Jesus] had won the victory in prayer while alone with God and was enabled to drive the devil back.

Another time after He had been alone in the mountains praying, a great storm came and the disciples thought the ship was about to go down, He calmed the tempest and the sea became as glass.

And in this lesson during this fast in the mountain He was alone with God all night in prayer. He was not talking to the wind, but in the ears of His Father, the God of heaven. He was about to undertake to do something requiring great wisdom and mighty power from God. He was about to select the pillars that were going to establish the Church of Christ—the Church of the living God.

So Jesus Christ could not be hid and if you are filled with God like you ought to be you can not be hid either. He could not be hid and when He came out of His hiding place He saw the disciples and a great multitude that were watching and waiting for Him. He called the disciples together to do a mighty work. He had many thousands following who had been healed and wonderfully blessed and who knew a great deal about the Son of God, so He had a mighty responsibility to choose the right ones. So He selected twelve and ordained them. He clothed them with power—He gave them license from heaven—God given authority—He filled them with the Holy Ghost—He loaned them the same power that He had over all devils and all unclean spirits and told them to go out two by two and preach the same Gospel He was preaching in the same way and exercise the same faith. He had exercised with God—cast out devils, heal the sick. He qualified them and ordained them with power from on high to go forth to accomplish the same results that He had. This was wonderful and all the disciples went down further into the plains.

We are told that great multitudes followed Him from Judea—a multitude is not less than five hundred people—and multitudes came out of all Judea and Jerusalem and from the sea coast of Tyre and Sidon and all along the sea coast out of towns and from every direction. There must have been many thousands out there in the hot sun. What did they come for? They came to hear Jesus, not just to get healed like some of you. They came to hear about Jesus—to get acquainted with Him—to see Him Whom to know is life eternal. They came to hear the Word that He brought from heaven—to find out the way that they might be saved and healed. They had a wonderful meeting there. Remember, they came to hear the Word and to see. Faith cometh by hearing—hearing the Word of God. How can they hear the Word of God without a preacher and how can he preach the Word of God unless God has sent him? How are people to get faith today to be healed when you preach against it? How will they get faith about the coming of the Son of God when you don't talk about it? Faith cometh by hearing the Word of God. No man can get down into the mysteries without the enlightening power of the Holy Ghost. If the Bible is sealed it is sealed to those that are lost—who are blinded by the god of this world. But this glorious Gospel brings you into communication with Jesus—God Almighty's dear Son—and with the Father that sent Him.

A Divine Healing Meeting

So these people were gathered there to hear and get acquainted with Jesus and to find the way to be healed. He took these disciples, the first thing after they were ordained for the ministry, into the greatest revival He ever held and gave them a start for the great work they had to do and it was a divine healing meeting from start to finish. Jesus Christ preached the glad tidings, salvation for the soul and healing for the body and redemption for the body. He preached the double cure—otherwise His fame never would have gone out over that country. They heard of the great physician, of His mighty love and power. No case was too hard for Him. No one too poor nor too rich if they came in God's way, He healed every one and not only healed but also saved, for He gave them the double cure. Himself took our infirmities and bare our sicknesses and by His stripes we are healed today.

Which is easier to say, Thy sins are forgiven thee, or to say to this paralytic, get up and walk? One is as easy as the other. Both miracles— God's power being demonstrated—the same power saves the soul and heals the body and will take us up to glory—make us so light we will rise without wings. Hallelujah!

So the Lord preached the Word to these people and they were healed, every one. Son, thy sins are forgiven thee—go and sin no more lest a worse thing come upon thee. Go and tell your friends, every one, what great things the Lord hath done. Don't forget it. Don't be so forgetful of His benefits. Serve God, give glory to God and that disease will never come back any more. Go—thou art whole. Go and sin no more lest it comes back and you die or something worse comes. Glory to God. You must see how much glory God is to get out of this. Hallelujah! So when He healed the body He saved the soul.

So all classes gathered in the plains, came out to see Jesus. Did you come here to see Jesus, or did you come here out of curiosity? I hope if you came through curiosity you are satisfied by this time. They came to see Jesus, get acquainted and hear the blessed doctrine He was preaching. Came to learn the way and to get this great salvation. It cost such an awful price, but God is offering it to you without money. Glory to God—accept it.

Shocks From the Heavenly Battery

These disciples were initiated in a great revival. Jesus preached as never man preached. He preached the glad tidings, salvation from sin and healing from their diseases. He preached the Word and made it plain and gave them to understand that whosoever will may come. O you nervous people, you who are going to have an operation. God can keep you from all these things. "I am the God of all flesh." Is there anything too hard for Jesus? No. He can move the mountain of tumor in a minute—move the cancer—soothe your nerves. You who are afraid the excitement will make you nervous, get a shock from the battery of heaven and you will sleep like a baby. He is the very same Jesus, the wonderworking Jesus, the same yesterday, today and forever. Glory! I am a witness.

So He went out to preach—and He did not have a lot of music, no pianos—but the power of God was there. It is not so much music, not so much singing—not such long prayers—not so much preaching, but the Spirit of the living God. So as He opened His mouth He spake as never man spake, because there was something back of it. He said, My Word is like the hammer that breaks the hard rock—like coals of fire on the brain, lodged in the heart, arrows dipped in the blood of Jesus, shot out by the lightning of God's power—strike men in the forehead and they fall like dead men.

The City of Destruction

Move out of the city of destruction, move to the cross, get out of the plains and start for glory tonight. They had a wonderful meeting there. So He preached the Word, showed them it was for them, showed them how to come, showed them what they had to do and they met the conditions. Every last one of them had to believe on Jesus and get close enough to touch Him.

Some one touched me—Glory. How do you know? I felt the virtue going out. You touch Jesus Christ with faith and God will come if He has to bring heaven down. It isn't the long prayer, nor the flowery prayer, but the prayer of faith. Faith that touches God and brings heaven down. Hallelujah!

The preaching was over, the altar call given and they began to make their way to Jesus, and they stood on the watch. Faith comes by watching, faith comes by hearing the wonderful testimonies they hear right here. We see them trying to come, trying to get there first, and every one that came received and if they had faith it did not take two or three hours for the flashlight to come from heaven.

These people accepted it. They did not carry their sick back over those plains in the hot sun, but they touched Him and the diseases went out and the demons went out like dogs and the healing virtue of Jesus went in and their bodies were healed and they went out to bring in others. Is that what you are doing? Or are you sitting down and waiting for it to come back? Bless the Lord.

So faith grew into knowledge. When they went they heard, but now they knew it was so. They saw it before their eyes; saw them running, leaping and skipping in every direction, and the excitement, as you call it, ran high and every one got in the battle and when you begin to get your eyes on Jesus Christ, you can tell it. So their faith grew and pretty soon they said we will just all rush there and the whole congregation—thousands of people —made a rush to try to touch the Son of God, and every one that touched Him was made whole. He cast out devils—you deaf spirit, you dumb spirit—come out. Jesus Christ came to destroy the works of the devil. So the multitude tried to touch Him and every one got the double cure, salvation for the soul and body. Got joy in their heart. Don't you believe it? Praise the Lord! So this was a great revival. He cast out the demons—and those possessed with devils will do all kinds of foolish, devilish things to torment every one.

But when Jesus came they knew they had to go out and they will have to go out if you come right. You have just as much power to cast out devils in the Name of Jesus Christ and the devils will run like a lot of dogs. Resist the devil and he will flee from you. But you have to keep them out or they will try to get in again. You keep them out. The maniac represents the Tribulation. The man had these devils all his life. Jesus says, you come out of him, and don't you ever come in any more. But He will cast the devils out of you and you have to keep them out yourself. Get the house full of [the] glory of God and give the Lord the key and you will not be bothered any more.

The Double Cure

This was a glorious meeting and Jesus initiated His disciples there to give them courage and they went out with gladness filled with the Spirit of mighty power and they went into the villages and cities and preached the Gospel—the double cure. They had never heard it before, but they preached the Gospel and healed the sick everywhere. Wherever they preached the double cure somebody believed and was healed. If they had not preached it no one would have known anything about it. Glory to God! You find this all through the Word of God and the greatest work that Jesus ever did was the healing of sick and the casting out of devils.

We are told that Jesus Christ was anointed by the Lord and began to preach and heal the sick of all kinds of diseases, for God was with Him. He was anointed of God to do this. Preach the Gospel and demonstrate it and prove it to be from God by healing the sick. Wherever He went He did that. The greatest revivals in the New Testament after Pentecost were the direct results of one or more divine healings of the body. The greatest victory in the Word of God to draw people to Christ. Nearly all the great revivals were brought about by divine healing and sometimes only one was healed. The man at the Beautiful Gate was healed and got the double cure. They were just going in to preach. The result was five thousand men were converted that day and Peter and John were thrown into prison. If you are all right you are going to be persecuted. But they began to shout and rejoice; they had results and were willing to lay in prison when they thought of the souls saved. Hallelujah!

Hundreds have been healed here. Look how hard your hearts are! You would not believe God if He walked over the platform. May God sweep away this damning sin of unbelief. We find that the same power Jesus had He gave to His disciples, He ordained seventy and sent them out. He first chose twelve and a few days later He chose seventy and gave them power over all kinds of devils. They went out and had great success and as soon as they believed Jesus Christ they had power. The Word was demonstrated by signs and wonders following and so God's Word must be demonstrated today. All through the Word, from Genesis to Revelation, whenever God gave a message to one or two—the message looked very foolish from the human standpoint and it took wonderful faith to go out and carry the message, but they knew God and whenever they went out and carried a message in God's way something happened. The Lord God came in a visible way with signs from heaven that all the people could see. God demonstrated that message. So these visible signs of the Spirit are the Word demonstrated.

Demons of Witchcraft and Sorcerism

The working of God's Spirit is foolishness to man. You go to some mesmerist or spiritualist and let them call up the dead and they can pull the wool over your eyes and you would rather believe that than believe Jesus Christ. They always try to counterfeit the real, don't they? God works today and the devil works. Back there there were witches and sorcerers, but God's people knew God and all through the Old Testament God demonstrated His Word. They acted like crazy people, but God was with them. He always came to the rescue and those that laugh last laugh best. The result was the fire of God fell on the people. They thought these men must be connected with heaven.

So the working of the Holy Ghost is foolishness to the natural mind. He is not discerned by the natural man, but you go to God and get the oil of heaven and you will have light on the Blessed Word of God and God will talk to your heart and Christ will be real and salvation will be real and heaven will be real because the Spirit of God will let you down into the deep things of God. Glory to God!

It was so on the Day of Pentecost when the Holy Ghost came. They said these are drunk. They lied about the Holy Ghost and they have been lying ever since, but the work went on just the same. Glory to God! They have always persecuted the work of God and grieved the Holy Ghost and treated the blood as something unholy.

If you don't know, if you don't believe, if you don't understand, ask God about these things. Don't go to some old infidel. Go to God. But you say as they did then: What do you think of it? Have any of the scribes believed? That is what they said before. Have any of our smart men believed yet?

You better believe in Christ, seek the wisdom that comes from above. He will make you wise in spiritual things. They are foolishness in the sight of man—but the wisdom of God, the things of God are eternal and they are what will take us to heaven.

I praise God for this wonderful salvation. I want to say a few words more about the work I know about. I have been standing before the public for forty years and God has given me grace and courage to stand. I have preached the Gospel in nearly every denomination. Thousands have gone out as ministers and workers. Many saints have gone home to glory.

We have been praying for the sick. If you have read my book you will remember when I started out I did not know I would have to pray for the sick, but I was sick and God healed me and raised me from a death bed. My friends said, "Somehow, I believe God is going to raise you up." I did not look like it, but I knew inside God wanted me to do something. I promised God if He would raise me up and show me His way I would do it. I started out after God baptized me in the Holy Ghost. I knew God was calling me for public service. I knew I would die unless God came to me like He did to the fishermen. I told the Lord if He would baptize me with power and knowledge that I would undertake the work. I would go to the ends of the earth and live a thousand years if I might take one soul to heaven. So the Lord wonderfully baptized me and sent me out. I did not try to heal then—don't now. God does the healing, but after a while God showed me I must pray for the sick. I had a big battle—nearly lost my soul before I would consent. He had to give me power—Bless God. He did. After that I began to pray for the sick. The devil kept telling me, "O you go to praying for the sick and they will bring wagon loads and nobody will be saved—and that is what you started out for"—and I felt that was so. When God comes, the devil comes. I fought about three nights and I was holding meetings in a big skating rink. About three nights I laid awake, but I thought God knew

His own business; so I said, "Lord, if You want me to pray You send them to me and by the grace of God I will do it." Since that time thousands and thousands have been saved through the healing that never would have been saved—they might have died in their sins. Dear friends, the people came, got convicted and saved and healed. I have been in Chicago three times and some of you know they came by hundreds rushing down the balconies, sides and aisles. The altar was full from one side to another. Every one trying to get there first. The whole place was crowded and people tried to get in the back way.

The Biggest Cripple There

The first meeting in the big stone church many hundreds came to be healed and saved and they came so thick and fast I could not stand it, so I told the preachers they had to commence. I called a brother and said, "You take this chair and pray for the sick." He said, "O I can't pray for the sick." I said, "Yes you can. I will pray for you." He said, "Give me an easy one." I gave him the biggest cripple I could find. Never mind, God can heal that cripple as easy as any. They thought they were in for it. We had five chairs standing on that great platform and two or three ministers to pray for the sick, but you would be surprised to see how many were healed. It is Jesus that does it. When a few were healed they had faith for the next one and it is wonderful how those people jumped and ran, shouting and praising God. Soon we had five rows of chairs and I would go back and forth and encourage them. God did mighty works. The next place we go we expect to see them coming by hundreds. Sometimes the power is so great when the saints are in one accord. People who are afflicted come from St. Louis, California, Alabama, and all over, and some come bringing their grave clothes along, but never one died yet that we know of. Jesus is a mighty Savior. Sometimes the power has been so great that I would go along great long altars telling them—I have no time to talk much. You know what to expect. The power of God is here. You give everything to God. In a few minutes they would be leaping and running in all directions.

The power of God will go out like rivers of water and if you are looking to God in faith you can get your baptism without waiting two or three weeks. It is not men or women, but God that does the work. Jesus Christ is the divine healer, baptizer. God gave Him power to give life to everyone that will come in God's way. In one meeting they came by hundreds and we never could get around and the power of God was so great, but we sprinkled the blood on them by faith and looked to God and we only had two or three minutes and fifty or one hundred trying to come up. It was so late, I said, the power of God will come if you believe. I said, by faith Moses took the blood of lambs and sprinkled the people and I take the blood of the real lamb, Calvary's Lamb, by faith, and sprinkle it over the people. I asked God to rebuke these diseases and take away their sins and right there the power of God fell in every direction. God did the work. Oh! Glory to God, who has given such wonderful powers to His church, through Jesus Christ, our Lord.

Chapter 5

The Power of the Word
When Demonstrated
in the Spirit

WHOSOEVER THEREFORE SHALL BE ASHAMED OF ME AND OF my words in this adulterous and sinful generation; of him also shall the Son of man be ashamed, when he cometh in the glory of his Father with the holy angels (Mark 8:38).

In the beginning was the Word, and the Word was with God, and the Word was God.

The same was in the beginning with God.

All things were made by him; and without him was not any thing made that was made.

And the Word was made flesh, and dwelt among us (John 1:1-3, 14).

That which was from the beginning, which we have heard, which we have seen with our eyes, which we have looked upon, and our hands have handled, of the Word of life;

(For the life was manifested, and we have seen it, and bear witness, and shew unto you that eternal life, which was with the Father, and was manifested unto us;)

That which we have seen and heard declare we unto you, that ye also may have fellowship with us: and truly our fellowship is with the Father, and with his Son Jesus Christ" (1 John 1:1-3).

The words of God have been sent down from heaven to us by Jesus Christ, and the holy apostles, spoken with the Holy Ghost. They are from God and go forth a living power.

Believest thou not that I am in the Father, and the Father in Me? the words that I speak unto you I speak not of myself: but the Father that dwelleth in me, he doeth the works.

Believe me that I am in the Father, and the Father in me: or else believe me for the very works' sake (John 14:10-11). They testify that the Father is in Me, and with Me (John 10:38, author's paraphrase).

God spake the worlds into existence. God said, "Let there be light," and there was light. As He spake the Word, the earth, land, light, darkness, the mighty seas, lakes, mountains, valleys with all the fruits and flowers sprang into life, into existence and beauty. He spake the Word and every living creature stood before Him; from the mighty monsters of the sea, the lion of the forest, wild beasts of every kind, down to the little singing bird, they stood looking in wonder and awe, at the Mighty God, that had by the Word of His mouth, and the power of His voice, called them into this beautiful world: saying by their very presence, "We know thou art the great Jehovah! the God that inhabitest Eternity."

Spake as Man Never Spake

When the high priest sent the officers to bring Jesus, the question was asked them, "Why did you not bring Him?" They said, "Never man spake like this man" (John 7:46). With His voice the dead are raised, the lepers cleansed; the blind see, they have their sight restored. The raging storm on the Sea of Galilee was hushed at His Word, and the roaring sea became as a sea of glass.

The words of God spoken by the Holy Ghost have the same effect today. There is as much power in the Name of Jesus today. Through the Holy Ghost, His words come like coals of fire, burning through the brains and hearts of men. They are shot out like arrows dipped in the blood of Jesus: like lightning, piercing the king's enemies in the head, and lodging in the heart: they fall like dead men. They are like David's little pebbles, we throw them at a venture, and God directs them so that they never return void. But they bring life, or death; heaven or hell. They stand forever, for by The Word we will be justified or condemned.

When the disciples were arrested and put into prison, as recorded in the fifth chapter of Acts, verses 19 and 20, "The angel of the Lord by night opened the prison doors, and brought them forth, and said, Go right back, stand in the temple, and speak all the words of this life" (author's paraphrase). You see God sent the angel to set them free, and to tell them to go back, amidst all their threats, and the danger, and to preach all the words of this life. His words are life, do not hold back any of the message.

Jesus says, "Whosoever shall be ashamed of me, and my words, of Him shall I be ashamed when I come in all the glory of the Father." Oh!

God help all that pretend to preach the Word, to see what is at stake. Will you please men or God? Will you deceive the people and come up at the judgment, with your hands dripping with the blood of souls?

Defiled With Blood

Behold, the Lord's hand is not shortened, that it cannot save: neither his ear heavy, that it cannot hear.

For your hands are defiled with blood, and your fingers with iniquity; your lips have spoken lies, your tongue hath muttered perverseness.

The way of peace they know not; and there is no judgment in their goings: they have made them crooked paths: whosoever goeth therein shall not know peace (Isaiah 59:1,3,8).

You have given them smooth sayings, trusting to good works, and a moral life. "In vain do ye worship me, teaching the doctrines, and traditions of men," that will perish with the using.[1]

Jesus says what He will do when He comes in all His glory. Yes, He is coming soon. This is the time of the end, we see the signs everywhere. In this wicked and adulterous generation, in these last days, the churches have gone after the wisdom and power of men, instead of the wisdom and power of God. "Having a form of godliness, but denying the power thereof: from such turn away" (2 Timothy 3:5). Read the third chapter of the second epistle of Timothy.

God is calling as never before, in thunder tones, to those who pretend to preach His Word, to "Blow the Trumpet in Zion," and to "Sound an alarm in the Holy Mountain." Let all the people tremble. What is the signal to make the people tremble? The Day of the Lord is at hand. It is even at your doors.

Blow ye the trumpet in Zion, and sound an alarm in my holy mountain: let all the inhabitants of the land tremble: for the day of the Lord cometh, for it is nigh at hand (Joel 2:1).

The great day of the Lord is near, it is near, and hasteth greatly, even the voice of the day of the Lord: the mighty man shall cry there bitterly.

That day is a day of wrath, a day of trouble and distress, a day of wasteness and desolation, a day of darkness and gloominess, a day of clouds and thick darkness, A day of the trumpet and alarm against the fenced cities, and against the high towers.

And I will bring distress upon men, that they shall walk like blind men, because they have sinned against the Lord: and their blood shall be poured out as dust, and their flesh as the dung.

Neither their silver nor their gold shall be able to deliver them in the day of the Lord's wrath; but the whole land shall be devoured by the fire of his jealousy: for he shall make even a speedy riddance of all them that dwell in the land (Zephaniah 1:14-18).

It Pays to Endure Till the End

Hear the angel shout, "The hour of his judgment has come. Repent and worship God, that made heaven, and earth, and the sea, and all that are therein" (Revelation 14:7, author's paraphrase).

The time has come when men will not endure sound doctrine, but turn the people to cunningly devised fables, turning away from the truth. Men of corrupt minds, reprobates concerning the truth, having a form of godliness, but denying the power thereof: From such turn away, for of him will I be ashamed when I come in all My glory. The last invitation is going forth, "Come to the marriage of the Lamb, and to the supper of the Lamb." The Gospel of His coming kingdom is being preached, as a witness to all nations. This work will soon be done. What are you doing? Preach all the words of this life. Oh! What a calling. Oh! What a privilege. The angels that stand before the throne cannot do this work.

Jesus said, "Tarry ... until ye be endued with power from on high" (Luke 24:49). "Ye shall receive power, after that the Holy Ghost is come upon you" (Acts 1:8). Then you shall cast out devils, ye shall speak with new tongues, take up serpents, or drink deadly poison, and they will not hurt you. You shall lay hands on the sick, and they shall recover. They shall have visions. Tell them, Jesus is coming soon. Show them the signs. The wise shall know the times. The wise shall shine as the firmament. They shall reign, be kings, with kingly authority, and bless the people as priests, for one thousand years.

The Bridal City

Do you not think that it will pay to be a true messenger, or herald, of His soon coming, when we shall be like Him, and shall have glorious bodies like His? "Of such will I be well pleased when I come in all my Father's glory." Oh! Can you not understand, He is coming as a Prince of Glory, to meet his bride in the air: to escort His bride back to the great City, to be present at the wedding, at the marriage of the Lamb, when Jesus will present His bride to the Father. He will welcome His Son's wife. He is coming in all the glory of all His holy angels. Oh! What a picture. Oh! What brightness. See, oh! see, the shining hosts! Gabriel that stands before God! Oh! They are getting ready! They are tuning up the heavenly choir. They are coming! They are coming to meet us in the air! For the Lord Jesus Himself shall descend from heaven with a shout, with the voice of the archangel, and with the trump of God: And the dead in Christ shall rise first (See 1 Thessalonians 4:16). They will come in the clouds of glory. We will all be caught up; changed in a moment; have glorious bodies like our Lord and Savior, Jesus Christ; to be forever with the Lord. Oh, this is wonderful, but it is true.

Oh! Dear Brethren in the ministry, can we miss this eternal weight of glory? When Jesus comes will He be ashamed of us? The wicked will be completely ignored, and banished from the Lord, from His glorious presence forever for being ashamed of Christ, or of His words, or of His supernatural and divine power, or of the works of the Spirit, that are foolishness to the world, and to the natural man. Will you miss all, for a high position, or a high salary, or a social position, or to please the people?

Oh! What can you do in that day?

Oh! God help us to preach all the words of this life, and earnestly contend for the faith once delivered to the saints.

As God sent Jesus into the world to deliver His messages, so Jesus sends us into the world, as his ministers, to preach the Gospel faithfully. Woe to us if we do not preach the whole truth, or are ashamed, or offended at any of His mighty works.

> Though we, or an angel from heaven, preach any other gospel unto you than that which we have preached unto you, let him be accursed.

> As we said before, so say I now again, If any man preach any other gospel unto you than that ye have received, let him be accursed.

> For do I now persuade men, or God? or do I seek to please men? for if I yet pleased men, I should not be the servant of Christ.

> But I certify you, brethren, that the gospel which was preached of me is not after man.
>
> For I neither received it of man, neither was I taught it, but by the revelation of Jesus Christ (Galatians 1:8-12).

Hear him say he was taught by the revelation of Jesus Christ, by inspiration, no man had taught him. You see the Bible is a sealed book to those that are lost. No one can preach the Gospel only [except] by inspiration and revelation by the Holy Ghost through Jesus Christ, for He takes the things of God and brings them to us; the Lord reveals them to us by His Spirit. "For the Spirit searches all things, yea, the deep things of God" (1 Corinthians 2:9-10). "But God hath revealed them unto us by His Spirit." With man's wisdom you can only learn historical knowledge, and the dead letter that kills and condemns; but the Spirit gives life and power; takes into the heart and mind thoughts from our loving Father, who says He will reveal His secrets to His sons! Jesus and the Father will come in and abide with us, and manifest themselves to us. Oh! Brother, do not handle the Word of God deceitfully, but as in the sight of God, we will preach the Word in the light and power of the Holy Ghost. Paul is our example; we should follow Paul as he followed Christ. "I was with you in weakness, and in fear, and in much trembling. And my speech and my preaching was not with enticing words of man's wisdom, but in demonstration of the Spirit and of power" (1 Corinthians 2:3-4). "For the gifts and calling of God are without repentance" (Romans 11:29).

This song was composed by a minister, sitting in the congregation, from a sermon preached on "The Great Day of His Wrath," twenty-seven years ago:

> In the awful day that's coming,
> > When Gabriel's trump shall sound
> And call the world to judgment,
> > Oh! where shall we be found?
> Shall we cry for the rocks and the mountains
> > To hide us in that day,
> From Him who comes in glory
> > With all His bright array?
>
> The Lord is coming shortly,
> > According to His word,
> Taking vengeance on the wicked

And them that know not God.
Oh! who will then be able
   In that awful day to stand?
"Thou shalt be no longer steward!"
   Will be the stern command.

Shall we begin to tremble
   While looking on that sight
And take our march in anguish
   Down to eternal night?
Oh! what an awful picture!
   To some it will come true;
And, Oh! my brother, sister,
   Shall it be I or you?

Chapter 6

The Prayer of Faith
Shall Save the Sick

IS ANY SICK AMONG YOU? LET HIM CALL FOR THE ELDERS OF the church; and let them pray over him, anointing him with oil in the name of the Lord:

And the prayer of faith shall save the sick, and the Lord shall raise him up; and if he have committed sins, they shall be forgiven him.

Confess your faults one to another, and pray one for another, that ye may be healed. The effectual fervent prayer of a righteous man availeth much.

Elias was a man subject to like passions as we are, and he prayed earnestly that it might not rain: and it rained not on the earth by the space of three years and six months (James 5:14-17).

The apostle James sends this letter out over the world to all churches, ministers and to every member of the body of Christ. All these teachings and blessings are for every child of God that will accept them. He wants the church to know that the power to heal the sick, and teach divine healing, was not confined to the apostles, but elders of each and every church had the gift of healing or the power to heal; and that by meeting the conditions given every one of the followers of Christ would positively be healed.

He delivered this doctrine of divine healing of the body to be taught and practiced in every church, that each member would know their privilege and duty to God. If he or she were sick, instead of sending for a doctor, perhaps an infidel doctor, they should send at once for the elder and let God glorify himself by manifesting the healing power in raising him up.

Some teachers refuse to walk in the God-given light and say this text means "Spiritual healing." I am glad the Word of God is so plain that anyone who wants the light can have it. "The prayer of faith shall save the sick and the Lord shall raise him up, and if he has committed sins they shall be forgiven him." You see the line between the raising up of the sick one, and the forgiving of sin. If they backslid, or sinned in any way that brought on the sickness, the sick ones should have faith in the promises of God in sending for the elders, as God had commanded.

The elders come and anoint with oil; a symbol of the Holy Ghost or healing virtue, that must come from Jesus, on and through the sick one—soul and body. They pray together, the prayer of faith, and having met the conditions, the Lord honors the faith, and comes with His mighty power and raises up the sick one to health and restores to him peace and joy in his soul. "Pray one for another that you may be healed."

You see the power of the Lord is ever present with His children to heal. The command is given to every child of God. If the elder cannot come, then get a few of God's children together in the true Spirit of Christ, and pray for one another, that you may be healed.

Some have gifts of casting out devils and healing, by laying on of hands. Oh! let us not forget these blood bought benefits. He forgiveth all our iniquities, He healeth all our diseases. He promises to heal soul and body; the verb is in the present tense. "The effectual, fervent prayer of a righteous man availeth much."

Unwavering Faith

The Lord shows us that we must have the righteousness of Christ, meet every other condition, and ask the Lord for what we want, in faith, without wavering. If we waver, or doubt, we need not expect anything, for God will not hear us.

The prayer of faith God will answer, if He had to bring all heaven down; to prompt us to greater faith, to ask the Lord for greater things.

He refers us back to the dark days of dearth and condemnation in which Elijah lived, and says, "He was a man, subject to like passions, as we are." He was not an angel, but a man, with the same human nature and passion as we have. He prayed earnestly, that it might not rain, and the heavens were shut up for three years and six months; he prayed again, and the rain came. He prayed for God to send fire from heaven, that the people might know there was a true God, and that he was God's servant, and the Lord was leading him.

The Lord wants us to ask for great signs and wonders. The fire that came from heaven, and brought the people down before God was a symbol of the Holy Ghost. The Lord wants to send into our midst signs and wonders, in answer to our prayers.

Elijah represents Christ—the Church. When Elijah was taken up to heaven, a double portion of his spirit came upon Elisha, and Elisha did many more signs and wonders than Elijah did.

"Verily, verily, I say unto you, He that believeth on me, the works that I do shall he do also; and greater works than these shall he do; because I go unto my Father. And whatsoever ye shall ask in my name, that will I do, that the Father may be glorified in the Son. If ye shall ask any thing in my name, I will do it" (John 14:12-14). "If ye abide in me, and my words abide in you, ye shall ask what ye will, and it shall be done unto you" (John 15:7).

You see, Christ's will and our will come together, with the same desire to glorify the Father. The Spirit of Christ prompting us to ask for great things, that the Lord will have a chance to let down His right hand of power, and let the people see the visible signs of the Lord of Hosts, that dwelleth in Zion.

Every one of us ought to be anointed with the same power and gifts that God hath set in the church, that the world may believe that the Father has sent Christ into the world, and that the Father hath loved us, as He loved him—Christ. "In my name shall they cast out devils; ...they shall lay hands on the sick, and they shall recover" (Mark 16:17-18).

These are the special gifts. I praise the Lord! He hath given these gifts to me. And in His Name, through His name, thousands of unclean spirits are cast out. The deaf, dumb, lame, blind, paralytic, and cancer devils have been driven out. Thousands of diseases have fled by laying on my hands, in His Name, and they were made whole.

Healing in the Atonement

Divine healing is taught in the Atonement, as much as the salvation of the soul. Isaiah, chapter 53, says: "He was wounded for our transgressions, he was bruised for our iniquities: the chastisement of our peace was upon him; and with his stripes we are healed" (v. 5).

Matthew 8:17, says: "That it might be fulfilled which was spoken by Esaias the prophet, saying, Himself took our infirmities, and bare our sicknesses."

"For by one Spirit are we all baptized into one body... ye are the body of Christ" (1 Corinthians 12:13, 27).

God has set some in the church or body: Firstly, apostles; secondarily, prophets; thirdly, teachers.

> For to one is given by the Spirit the word of wisdom; to another the word of knowledge by the same Spirit;
>
> To another faith by the same Spirit; to another the gifts of healing by the same Spirit;
>
> To another the working of miracles; to another prophecy; to another discerning of spirits; to another divers kinds of tongues; to another the interpretation of tongues" (1 Corinthians 12:8-10).

Together we have the promise of apostles, prophets, teachers and evangelists, in the coming Church of Christ. What a glorious church, is the real body and bride of our Lord!

The signs were to follow their works:

"For the perfecting of the saints, for the work of the ministry, for the edifying of the body of Christ" (Ephesians 4:12).

You see that God placed all the gifts and working of the Spirit in the church and they were to remain with the people of God, "Till all come in the unity of the faith by the same Spirit. To every man is given the manifestation of the Spirit to profit withal; but all these worketh the selfsame Spirit—One Lord and one Spirit."[1]

The Holy Ghost is the agent of Christ, sent by God, to work through the church, the body of Christ, and each member is to possess one or more of these gifts, as we walk in the light and believe and accept these blessings, or gifts.

Ignorance Inexcusable

Paul says, "Concerning spiritual gifts, brethren, I would not have you ignorant, concerning the knowledge of the Son of God, till we all come in the unity of the faith unto a perfect man, unto the measure of the stature of the fullness of Christ."[2]

Dearly beloved, when will we all come up to this measure? Not until the last one of the little flock is ready to be translated. We must be filled with the fullness of God, with wisdom and power. These signs and gifts must follow until the Church goes out to meet the Lord —the

Bridegroom. She will go out to meet Him with the same power that the apostles had, after they were filled with the Holy Ghost on the Day of Pentecost. Oh! praise the Lord, all these signs are with us and are manifested in our meetings.

Chapter 7

Signs and Wonders
to Lead
People to Christ

WE ALL KNOW, WHO HAVE READ THE ACTS OF THE APOSTLES, that their ministry was marvelously successful. Here are a few brief reports of some of their revivals:

Then they that gladly received his Word were baptized: and the same day there were added unto them about three thousand souls (Acts 2:41).

Howbeit many of them which heard the word believed; and the number of the men was about five thousand (Acts 4:4).

And believers were the more added to the Lord, multitudes both of men and women (Acts 5:14).

Then had the churches rest throughout all Judaea and Galilee and Samaria, and were edified; and walking in the fear of the Lord, and in the comfort of the Holy Ghost, were multiplied (Acts 9:31).

While Peter yet spake these words, the Holy Ghost fell on all them which heard the word (Acts 10:44).

And the hand of the Lord was with them: and a great number believed, and turned unto the Lord (Acts 11:21).

And the next sabbath day came almost the whole city together to hear the word of God (Acts 13:44).

But the word of God grew and multiplied (Acts 12:24).

And so were the churches established in the faith, and increased in number daily (Acts 16:5).

And some of them believed, and consorted with Paul and Silas; and of the devout Greeks a great multitude, and of the chief women not a few (Acts 17:4).

And the word of God increased; and the number of the disciples multiplied in Jerusalem greatly; and a great company of the priests were obedient to the faith (Acts 6:7).

Therefore many of them believed; also of honourable women which were Greeks, and of men, not a few (Acts 17:12).

And the Lord added to the church daily such as should be saved (Acts 2:47).

And this was known to all the Jews and Greeks also dwelling at Ephesus; and fear fell on them all, and the name of the Lord Jesus was magnified.

And many that believed came, and confessed, and shewed their deeds (Acts 19:17-18).

Many Books Burned

Many of them also which used curious arts brought their books together, and burned them before all men: and they counted the price of them, and found it fifty thousand pieces of silver. So mightily grew the word of God and prevailed (Acts 19:19-20).

There are three reasons or causes that gave the disciples this phenomenal success:

First, they preached the Gospel of the kingdom, which is, as I have already stated, a full gospel for spirit, soul and body. They preached exactly as the Lord told Jeremiah to preach (Jeremiah 26:2).

Thus saith the Lord; Stand in the court of the Lord's house, and speak unto all the cities of Judah, which come to worship in the Lord's house, all the words that I command thee to speak unto them; diminish not a word.

And [they preached exactly] as He told Jonah to preach (Jonah 3:1-2):

And the word of the Lord came unto Jonah the second time, saying, Arise, go unto Nineveh, that great city, and preach unto it the preaching that I bid thee.

The apostles did not diminish a word of the Gospel of the kingdom. They preached precisely the Gospel that Christ bade them preach. And such preaching God will always honor and bless.

In the second place, they preached this Gospel under the power of the Holy Ghost. This they received on the Day of Pentecost. This is such an essential and all-important factor in preaching that Jesus would not permit them to enter upon their great lifework until they had received the divine anointing.

Had they not tarried in Jerusalem until this anointing came, there would never have been any Acts of [the] Apostles written, for there would not have been any acts upon their part needing to be recorded, and the revivals mentioned above would never have been reported.

In the third place, God bore witness to their preaching with signs and wonders and with divers miracles and gifts of the Holy Ghost. And this was as important a factor in their success as either of the others. I am satisfied that without these miracles the Gospel would have made but little progress in pushing its way through the heathen world.

Notice the apostles' prayer, which shows the estimation they placed upon miracles, especially the miracle of healing, as an auxiliary in their work:

> Acts 4:29-30: And now, Lord, behold their threatenings: and grant unto thy servants, that with all boldness they may speak thy word, By stretching forth thine hand to heal; and that signs and wonders may be done by the name of thy holy child Jesus.

Notice now a significant fact. Read the following:

> Acts 5:12, 15-16: And by the hands of the apostles were many signs and wonders wrought among the people....
>
> Insomuch that they brought forth the sick into the streets, and laid them on beds and couches, that at the least the shadow of Peter passing by might overshadow some of them.
>
> There came also a multitude out of the cities round about unto Jerusalem, bringing sick folks, and them which were vexed with unclean spirits: and they were healed every one.

The significant fact is, that in this passage is a parenthesis which reads as follows: ("and they were all with one accord in Solomon's porch. And of the rest durst no man join himself to them.... And believers were the more added to the Lord, multitudes both of men and women") [Acts 5:12-14].

Why did Luke insert that parenthesis? Did those miracles have anything to do with that multitude of believers, both men and women, being added to the Lord? They constituted a powerful factor in that revival.

That was the result in nearly every instance, where miracles were performed great revivals followed. Read these words:

> Acts 6:7-8: And the word of God increased; and the number of the disciples multiplied in Jerusalem greatly; and a great company of the priests were obedient to the faith.

And Stephen, full of faith and power, did great wonders and miracles among the people.

Is there any relation between the miracles that Stephen wrought and the multiplication of disciples in Jerusalem? There is a most intimate and vital relation.

Take another case:

Acts 8:5-8: Then Philip went down to the city of Samaria, and preached Christ unto them.

And the people with one accord gave heed unto those things which Philip spake, hearing and seeing the miracles which he did.

For unclean spirits, crying with loud voice, came out of many that were possessed with them: and many taken with palsies, and that were lame, were healed.

And there was great joy in that city.

Did the miracles of casting out unclean spirits and healing the lame have anything to do with the people giving heed with one accord to the things that Philip spake, and filling that city with joy? Very much.

Take another case:

Acts 9:32-35: And it came to pass, as Peter passed throughout all quarters, he came down also to the saints which dwelt at Lydda.

And there he found a certain man named Aeneas, which had kept his bed eight years, and was sick of the palsy.

And Peter said unto him, Aeneas, Jesus Christ maketh thee whole: arise, and make thy bed. And he arose immediately.

And all that dwelt at Lydda and Saron saw him, and turned to the Lord.

Raising Dorcas to life was another case with the same effect: "And it was known throughout all Joppa; and many believed in the Lord" (Acts 9:42).

If ministers could cast out devils today in the Name of Jesus, and lay hands on the sick and have them restored to health, they would not preach to empty benches, nor mourn over the dearth of revivals. On the contrary, every minister who could do that would have crowded houses and a perpetual revival. And that is what God wants His ministers to do, and it is not His fault if they are not able to do it.

There is nothing the devil hates with more infernal malignity than divine healing. That is something that is visible, tangible, real and valuable.

When a lame man is made to walk, or a poor epileptic made well, there is something the unsaved world can see and appreciate. And it convinces them of the goodness and loving kindness of God.

A book is lying before me entitled, "Back to the Bible." I see another advertised, "Back to Pentecost." Does it occur to these authors that to get back to the Bible and to Pentecost is to get back to miracle-working power?

Such a return would not only secure the Baptism of the Spirit, but it would secure the gifts of the Spirit in the working of miracles. Is there anyone taking the back track in that direction?

Chapter 8

The Closing
of the Gentile Age

THE LORD SHALL RISE UP AS IN MOUNT PERAZIM, HE SHALL BE wroth as in the valley of Gibeon, that he may do his work, his strange work; and bring to pass his act, his strange act.

Now therefore be ye not mockers, lest your bands be made strong: for I have heard from the Lord God of hosts a consumption, even determined upon the whole earth (Isaiah 28:21-22).

In all the history of the Bible, and in all God's dealings with the world, He sent and offered them mercy and deliverance first, and did everything to persuade them to trust and obey Him, and to escape the coming judgments. But they kept on sinning still, till the pent up wrath of God was poured out, and they were all destroyed. With a strong hand, and a supernatural power, He was with His people in the Spirit of judgment and of strength, to them that turned the battle to the gate.

When mercy ceased to be a virtue, judgments came like a desolation, and destruction like a whirlwind, and then hear Him say, "You will seek me right early, but your cries come too late, I will not answer. I will laugh at your calamities, and mock when your fear cometh" (Proverbs 1:26-28, author's paraphrase).

In all the threatened dangers, and in the midst of awful judgments, the Lord caused His supernatural presence to be seen in signs through His children; while showing wrath. He worked His strange work through, and by, the Holy Spirit.

With all these past warnings and examples of mercy, and awful calamities that came with, or followed the loving voice of God, so tenderly [calling them] from their evil ways, to fly to His outstretched arms; with all these past warnings and examples, the poor blinded, debauched world does not, and will not, take warning, but after six thousand years she keeps on sinning; still seems to take the management from God, saying, "God does not know, He does not care, we will run the machinery ourselves."

They are running wild after wealth, and form, worshipping the wisdom of men, and these mighty inventive powers. Even in their professed worship, they have left the Fountain Head of Living Waters, and have hewn out cisterns, broken cisterns, that will hold no water. They have turned their backs to God, and are facing the sun of human wisdom, and power that has risen, and blinded them, so that they are satisfied with the gods of this world.

Hear one of the last warning notes from the Eternal Throne from the loving Father: "In vain ye worship me, going after the doctrines, and traditions of men, which will perish with the using." [1]

The time of trifling is about over. God is calling the Elijah class, that are clothed with the power of God, and King Ahab to come face to face, and test their gods. We must come to a halt and put our gods to a test; and the one that answers by fire, will serve, that is God's test.

It shall come to pass, in the last days, saith the Lord, I will plead with all flesh, with the sword and fire, and the slain of the Lord shall be many (Isaiah 66:16, author's paraphrase).

The sword is the Word of God. The fire is the Holy Ghost. The slain of the Lord are those that fall under conviction, or like dead men and women, under the power of God.

Lightning of His Power

He will send out His arrows; His Word dipped in the blood of Jesus, shot out with the lightning of His power, and they shall wound the King's enemies in the head. They shall fall at His feet. Oh, praise His name, when God has His way the tent ground looks like a battlefield; men, women, and children lying in all parts, like dead men.

According to God's Word, the time of trouble, such as men have never seen, or known, or ever will see again, has already commenced, and will finish with the battle of the Great God.

We are in the last days of His preparation, and Jesus is coming soon for His bride (1 Thessalonians 4:16-17), and she is getting ready. He is sending His angels, His servants, with the sound of a trumpet calling the elect together, so that we may all be baptized with one faith, one Spirit and one mind; that we may be amongst the wise, that shall shine as the brightness of the firmament.

In the chapter from which the text is taken, which refers to the last or Laodicean church, which is the vine of the earth, the vine of man's planting, He shows that in the awful destruction in which she will be utterly destroyed, the saints who are going through, will be clothed with power.

The Lord will rise up as in Mount Perazim, He shall be wroth as in the Valley of Gibeon, that He may do His acts, His strange acts, that He may work and bring to pass His strange [works], in the Last Call of Mercy. He will stir up the elements. "Behold, the Lord hath a strong and mighty tempest, of hail, and destroying storms, of floods, of mighty waters overwhelming the earth" (Isaiah 28:2, author's paraphrase). He will bring distress upon men, because they have sinned against God, and their blood shall be poured out as dust, and their flesh as dung; neither shall their gold or silver be able to deliver them in the Day of the Lord's wrath. He will rise in His wrath and work His strange work.

He will help His saints today, as he did [David] at Mount Perazim, and [Joshua] at Gibeon. He will bring the powers of heaven, the destructive elements together, to accomplish His work through His saints. The hosts of the enemies had gathered against David. [See 1 Chronicles 14:8-17 and 2 Samuel 5:17-25]. He asked help of the Lord. The Lord told him not to go near them, but [to] take his forces back, and go under the mulberry trees, and to pay no attention to them, but to rest, and wait until he heard the sound of the going in the tops of the mulberry trees; then he should take his army and go forth to battle, and go after the enemy, for the Lord had gone before them, and He would smite the hosts of the Philistines....

The enemies heard the noise of the great hosts, the going in the tree tops, the sound of war, of approaching armies. God confused them, and they were frightened, for they thought that David had engaged all the armies in the land against them.

It took great faith for David to obey the voice of God, and to rest so careless under the trees, when the hosts of enemies were ready to destroy them, but he knew the battle was the Lord's, and that unless He fought for them, they were lost.

He was waiting for help from heaven, the armies of heaven were coming down to fight their battles, and they must wait till they heard the bugle blast, the rolling of chariots, the cannonading, and the noise of marching hosts. Oh, yes, our God of battles gave them the victory, and they fled before the Lord....

The enemy had gathered five kings with all their armies against Joshua. [See Joshua 10:1-27], and they were sure of victory. They were trusting to the arm of flesh, but the Mighty God of heaven was coming with His armies....

The Lord said to Joshua, "Fear them not, for I shall destroy them, shall deliver them into thy hand. There shall not a man stand before thee" (Joshua 10:8, author's paraphrase).

...The Lord followed them, and cast down great stones from heaven, so that more men died with the hail stones than by the sword.

He will work His strange work, as in Gibeon; the battle was on. The enemy was strong, defeat was sure; unless the God of Battles came to the rescue; the only hope was for God to work a miracle, to do a strange act.

The Lord told Joshua to command the sun to stand still, and the sun stood still in the midst of the heavens, not to go down for a whole day. And [He told him] to command the moon to stand still, and not to go down until they had gained a victory.

There was no day like it before, that the Lord hearkened to the voice of man. The Lord fought for them. He says He will rise up in wrath, and work His strange work, His strange acts, as He did in Gibeon, the whole land will be destroyed. He will make a speedy riddance of the whole land.

Two-thirds of the tribes of the earth will perish by storms, earthquakes, hail, cyclones, floods, pestilence, and famine, in this time of trouble. "And there fell upon men a great hail out of heaven, every stone about the weight of a talent (one hundred pounds or more): and men blasphemed God because of the plague of the hail; for the plague thereof was exceeding great" (Revelation 16:21).

God's Strange Acts

Since God is pouring out His Spirit in these last days (See Acts 2:17) of the Latter Rain, and His people are seeking and receiving the Baptism of the Holy Ghost, with all the Pentecostal gifts and blessings,

God has risen up, and is working His strange work, His strange acts, the acts of the apostles through God's baptized saints.

When the Holy Ghost came on the Day of Pentecost like a rushing wind, this was His Strange Act, like as His armies in the tree top.

When they saw the tongues of fire on the heads of the hundred and twenty disciples, and they were all filled with the Holy Ghost, and began to speak in other tongues as the Spirit gave utterance, this was God's strange act, His strange work.

While Peter was preaching at the home of Cornelius, the Holy Ghost was poured out on all, and they spake with new tongues and magnified God. This was His strange work, His strange act.

When the paralytic took up his bed and walked out, all the people shouted with a loud voice, giving glory to God. The fear of God fell on all. They walked softly, saying, "We have seen strange things today." Oh praise God. Praise His holy Name for ever and ever.

This is the day, this is the time spoken of. He has risen up in majesty, like a mighty man of power, and of war.

Hear the Spirit of the Conqueror, "Come up, my people, come up to the help of the Lord, against the mighty." The devil is mighty in these last days, but the battle is the Lord's.

It is not only against us the hosts have gathered, but against the Lord of Hosts. The Captain of the Lord's Hosts, He has come down to fight our battles. He is in our midst. He goes before us with a two-edged sword, He has bowed the heavens, and has come down. He is making the people tremble. He is moving the mountains of difficulty, and of sin, of tumors, and of cancers. He is tearing down the devil's works, and breaking the hearts of stone.

Yes, the Lord is bringing the powers of heaven and the destroying elements together. Rising up in His wrath.

When His judgments are in the earth some will repent. Yes, we see the great calamity, the sinking of the mighty ship (the S. S. "Titanic") causing travail, and gloom, and sorrow, and awakening the people all over the world. We see great loss of life in floods, fire, and earthquake.

We see the terrifying storms and cyclones. Men and women turn pale for fear, and looking, and wondering what will happen next. Yes the Lord is working with the elements, and the strange work of the Holy Ghost through His children. The great work of giving the Last

Warning, the Last Call to escape these things that are coming upon the earth, and to stand before the Lord at His coming. He is sending His angels, His saints, with the sound of a great trumpet.

The Gospel is the trumpet, and it is blown in Zion. "Sound the alarm in my Holy Mountain." Let all the people tremble. The great Day of the Lord is near, it is near, even at your doors. It is the Last Call to be saved, before the great and notable Day of the Lord come. "Therefore be ye not mockers, lest your bands be made strong: for I have heard from the Lord God of hosts a consumption, even determined upon the whole earth" (Isaiah 28:22).

We can all see the strange work, in the workings of the Holy Ghost through, and with, the baptized saints. "Concerning this sect,...every where it is spoken against" (Acts 28:22).

The workings of the Holy Ghost are foolishness to men. They cry out, and say, "They are drunken;" but not with wine or strong drink. They say, "They are hypnotized, and mesmerized." Many are mockers, they see the strange and supernatural with the natural eye, and hear with their ears the wonderful works of God. They confess there was and is, great power. They cannot deny the great miracles. It makes them fear and tremble; but many turn away, drive off conviction, and become mockers.

They commit the unpardonable sin, and their bands are made strong, they are lost forever. The Lord says He will consume them in His wrath. They will not mock then, when the cyclone is raging, when the earth is rocking and reeling under the earthquake. But now they make much sport, and say of the strange and supernatural, "It is true there is a work done, but it is the work of the devil."

Daniel in the vision heard one saint ask another, "When shall all these wonders cease?" The answer was "When He shall have accomplished to scatter the power of the holy people, all these wonders shall cease" (Daniel 12:6-7, author's paraphrase). The Gospel of His coming kingdom must first be preached, as a witness to all nations. God will have many witnesses out of every nation, tongue, and people on the earth.

Signs, Wonders and Works

These signs, wonders, works and demonstrations, and the power of the Holy Ghost, through the baptized saints, must be scattered. This is our work today, calling the elect together, that they may see, feel, and receive the baptism, and be sealed with the knowledge. That they may be among the wise that shall know when Jesus is coming, they shall shine as the sun in our Father's kingdom.

The Lord of Hosts is with us today, for a crown of glory, and a diadem of beauty unto the residue of His people, and with great power to those that press the battle to the gates.

He is giving His wisdom to the weak; to those who naturally have not the wisdom of this world, He is teaching knowledge and making us to understand. Those that are weaned from the milk; little children, and those who are not learned; and revealing and manifesting Himself to them. Yea, He reveals the deep things of God, speaking in new tongues, as the Spirit gives utterance, showing the wonderful works of God.

He is speaking in other languages fluently, plainly and distinctly, and with power, that which no one can learn at school, except after a long time. With stammering lips and other tongues will I speak unto this people, yet for all that you will not believe. Oh readers, be not mockers lest your bands be made strong, lest ye be consumed. Hear Him say so. Hear, brother.

Paul says, referring to this warning, hundreds of years after it was spoken in solemn warning by the prophet, that it is one of the last signs that God is giving to the lost world that God is moving in their midst, and that Jesus is coming. Yes, it is a special sign that Jesus is coming soon ([1 Corinthians 14:21]; 1 Thessalonians 4:16). Yet with all this you will not believe. Be careful how you hear; how you act. It is the Last Call. God is working His strange work and His strange act. The Holy Ghost is seen in many ways. He is seen in bright lights, in balls of fire, in hundreds of stars, and in bands of angels over, and in the tent in our meetings.

The Lord of Hosts says He will work, as He did when the sun and moon stood still at the command of Joshua. We will not be surprised at anything our God does. His people are a people of power. "All thy works shall praise thee, O Lord; and thy saints shall bless thee. They shall speak of the glory of thy kingdom, and talk of thy power" (Psalm 145:10-11).

Chapter 9

Will Ye Also
GO Away?

As the living Father hath sent me, and I live by the Father: so he that eateth me, even he shall live by me. This is that bread which came down from heaven: not as your fathers did eat manna, and are dead: he that eateth of this bread shall live for ever (John 6:57-58).

And if he keeps on eating and believing he shall never die spiritually. Many of the disciples said, "This is an hard saying; who can hear it?" (John 6:60). Jesus knew their murmuring and He gave them a little insight into the great resurrection. "What and if ye shall see the Son of man ascend up where he was before?" (John 6:62). He said, "Therefore said I unto you, that no man can come unto me, except it were given unto him of my Father" (John 6:65). That is a wonderful truth. No man ever made his way to Jesus without God. No man ever made his way to Jesus unless the Father sent His Spirit out and drew him.

From that day many of His disciples went back and walked no more with Him. Then said Jesus unto the twelve, Will ye also go away? I think He never was more sad. He saw the multitude turn away, they would not walk in the light. Simon Peter answered, "Lord, to whom shall we go? thou hast the words of eternal life. And we believe and are sure that thou art that Christ, the Son of the living God" (John 6:68-69). Many do not believe that today. Many do not know it, but that is the key to the whole Word of God. And we believe and are sure that Thou art the Christ, the Son of the living God. As the living Father has sent me and I live by the Father, so we must live the same way, by the power of the Almighty God. Glory to God.

We see by what we have heard, the Lord had many thousand followers by this time. His fame had gone out all over the land. He had five thousand converts when He supplied them with bread in the wilderness, and another time seven thousand who saw the mighty power of the Almighty God through Jesus Christ when they ate and were filled, and many baskets were taken up from what remained of the few loaves and fishes. Thousands came to Him for salvation and healing and when they were healed they got salvation always. He gave them the double cure. Which is easier, to take away sins or heal the body? One is as easy as the other. "Behold, thou art made whole: sin no more, lest a worse thing come unto thee" (John 5:14). They got the double cure, saved and healed. They were pretty well acquainted with the Christ and His love and mercy and mighty power. They heard of His fame and every day His power was greater and more wonderfully demonstrated. We find one day when the ship was going down and the waves were going over it and all were about to be drowned, when they had faith to come and call Him, He stepped out and said, "Peace be still." And the mighty wind ceased and the rolling waves suddenly became as a sea of glass through the mighty power of Christ. The mighty power of God fell upon the people and they came forward and said, "Behold, what manner of man is He any way? Is there no limit to His mighty power? This man, this Messiah, says he is the Son of God. We are following him from day to day and every day we see more of his mighty power. There is no limit to it, even the winds and the waves obey him." And all the ship fell at His feet and acknowledged Him as the Son of God. So His fame went everywhere, not so much by what He said, but because of the mighty manifestations.

"If you don't believe what I say, believe me for the works' sake. They are they which testify that I came from God and am the Son of the living God. Though I spake as never man spake, you have a cloak, but before the mighty signs and wonders you stand before God naked." They had seen the mighty miracles, heard Him speak, saw His majesty and power in so many ways, but now He began to turn, began to tell them about being filled with God, giving up to the fullness of God, being baptized with the Holy Ghost, being kept by the authority of God, and as He said, as by the living Father I live, by the living God He was sustained and kept continually by the power and presence of God, for the Father never left Him for a moment. He said, "The works that I do I do not do, but my Father doeth the works. The words I say, I do not say, but my Father gives me the words. Whatsoever the Father tells me to do I do." He gave the Father credit for everything.

As He was sustained by the mighty power of the living God, we must come to the point where we can be sustained and kept the same way, by the power of God through Jesus Christ. This is a hard saying— who can be saved? We are not to live by the natural bread alone, but to get to heaven we must have the spiritual man sustained and fed by the bread of heaven, sustained by the Holy Ghost. We need to drink from the fountain that never runs dry. But they did not understand and did not want to. So many don't want to walk in the light and they turn away and are lost forever. Who then can be saved? And they began to murmur and grumble as they do today. God knows when they grumble. Many thousands of those people that were saved and had all those blessings, turned away and never followed the Son of God any more. Jesus looked at the few left and His heart must have been broken for those who were so blind. And He is saying the same thing to us. While so many are backslidden and going off into delusions. It is the sifting time as never before. God is looking at us and especially those who are baptized. Will you also go away? Will you also forsake Me? Will you also turn back, or will you go forward all the way? Peter said, "To whom shall we go? We cannot find a better way. This has been a glorious way and we are willing to go all the way. Thou alone hast the words of eternal life. We don't guess —we know of a truth that thou art the Christ, the Son of the living God." Jesus said, "What if you see me ascend up to heaven?" He wanted to show them the mighty power of the Holy Ghost, resurrection life and the saints going up by the same power. "I am the living bread that cometh down from heaven, he that eateth me shall live by me and if he continues to eat he will never die spiritually."

They Laughed at the Signs

He said to the few who remained, "Will ye also go away?" And they answered, "We know of a truth that Thou are the Christ, the Son of the living God that you have been telling us about." Oh! glory to God! Dear friends, God's people were always the fewest of all the people on earth. He said to the children of Israel: I did not choose you because you were the wisest people, or the wealthiest people, but you were the fewest of all the people on the earth [Deuteronomy 7:7]. I have called you, chosen you, put my love upon you. We find the previous followers of the Lord always diminished instead of increased. We find way back from the beginning at the time of the flood when the ark finally sailed away, only eight souls had faith enough to sail away and all the rest went down to an awful doom. They saw the mighty signs and the mighty wonders, but they would not believe God, laughed at the sign, thought Noah was a fool and the ark was the craziest building they ever saw. They turned away after having had the light.

Even at the great conflagration on the plains when the judgments of God and the fire of God came down and destroyed these proud cities God even sent an angel from heaven to warn them, but only three souls escaped to the mountains. They had the chance; they had the opportunity, but they turned back, took the wrong way. God gave mercy first until finally His mercy ceased. They lost their opportunity, judgments came. Judgments always follow and always will follow the backslider who refuses to obey God. It is judgment unto death. Where Christ is they never can go. We find all through the Word of God there were just a few. At the destruction of Jerusalem they had the call, they all had a chance, but not many escaped.

Only Twelve Left

Now I want to come down to Christ, as I said before, after these multitudes went back and there were only twelve left, the question was asked: "Will ye also go away? Lord, to whom shall we go? Thou hast the words of eternal life." The rest never followed Him any more; we never hear of them. These people were saved, but they did not follow the Son of God any more. After He rose from the dead he appeared to his disciples, called for fish and ate it in their presence; called Thomas to come and put his finger into His side and proved to them that He had the same body that was laid in the grave. Many different times He appeared to them to take away every doubt and prove He was the risen Christ, the Son of the living God, and would soon ascend back to God where He came from. Different times He met with them and at one time He was seen of five hundred disciples after He arose from the dead. Many believe that this was the time He ascended on high when He went out on the mountain, talked to them the last time, gave the last commission and [they] watched Him ascending into heaven until the angels appeared and said, "Why stand ye gazing up into heaven? this same Jesus, which is taken up from you into heaven, shall so come in like manner as ye have seen him go into heaven" (Acts 1:11). And they remembered that He charged them, "Don't preach sermons, or teach the people or do anything, but tarry at Jerusalem until ye be endued with power from on high" (Luke 24:49, author's paraphrase). They had a great deal to preach about, of

Christ's sufferings, death and resurrection, but He told them, You have not entered into this wonderful life until you are endued with power from on high. Glory to God! I want you to see that Christ wanted to select men and women to set up His spiritual kingdom. He wanted to qualify them to establish the Holy Ghost religion in the world. But after all they had seen and heard and after these five hundred saw Jesus and they were thoroughly convinced that He was the Son of God, there were only one hundred and twenty out of the five hundred, to say nothing about any of the rest, that really believed and were willing to face the music, bear death or anything else, until God qualified and sent them out. See how His work had diminished after He was taken. God help you to see whose fault it was that they did not all come up there and tarry to be initiated into the Holy Ghost Baptism and the secrets of heaven. Only one hundred and twenty who believed that God would fulfill the promise made hundreds of years before to the prophets and confirmed by Jesus; and when the Day of Pentecost came there were only a little company there with God to be qualified to establish the Holy Ghost church. They were saved and full of joy; they believed they would receive the Holy Ghost and they went back to Jerusalem and tarried, continually blessing and praising God. They were filled with joy. Now you people who are seeking the Baptism, get saved first, get filled with joy, get off the judgment seat, be of one accord, of one mind, praising the Lord.

Blaze of Pentecostal Power

Christ's church was set up in a blaze of Pentecostal power. Common, unlearned men and women went there, trusting God, and the power of heaven came down. Suddenly, while they were praising and blessing God—they knew God was coming and they were not criticizing as to how He would come, but they were willing to leave that all in God's hands—and suddenly they heard a sound from heaven like a rushing, mighty wind and the whole building was shaken and the tidal wave filled the place, the power of God struck them and the Holy Ghost came and sat on each of them like tongues of fire. God was initiating them into the deep things of God and making them pillars in the Church of the Living God. This was where the church was established, where the church was organized, the Church of the First Born. Glory to God! And these were all that the Lord had to depend on to establish the church and spread the glad news of what had happened. "You shall receive power after the Holy Ghost has come upon you and then you shall know how to testify of Me. Tell them in a way that people will believe and I will be with you always and when you preach the Word you will see the signs of the living Christ right in your midst."

Glory to God! They began to preach the wonderful things, filled with the Holy Ghost, and the Lord Jesus Christ was with them. He was there invisible. He was coworker together with them, and He is working with His saints today. The Lord Jesus Christ confirms the Word with signs and wonders following.

But when the news went out and the crowds came to see what was taking place on the Day of Pentecost they said these people are all drunk. They began to lie about the Holy Ghost and they have been lying ever since. Peter took up the old prophets and said, You believe the prophets hear what they say, "This is that—just what they said was coming, what God said should take place in the last days." This which you see with the natural eye and this you hear—and we know they felt it—this is the power of God. It is the Holy Ghost sent down from heaven. But the great company that had followed Him before and saw the mighty miracles, refused to walk in the light. When we are born of the Spirit we have some of the light of heaven in our souls. Jesus is giving us more light and giving us degrees of glory. As long as we walk in that light we shall have fellowship with one another and the blood of Jesus Christ, His Son, cleanses us from sin. You are either going back or forward, but as long as we walk in that light we have fellowship and love for each other and have a present salvation, but when you refuse to walk in the light you go back and you lose that sweet fellowship with God and with the saints. God is testing us just like He did the Jews, down to the end of the age. "Fear not, little flock, it is your Father's good pleasure to give you the Kingdom" (Luke 12:32). He said He would never come unless there was a falling away. God knows there is a falling away today. The Church of Jesus Christ was inaugurated in a blaze of glory and celestial fire works, but she must be taken up in a greater blaze of glory. The Holy Spirit will continue to take us down into the deep things of God and we shall be filled with all the fullness of God, with our garments white and our lamps brightly burning. The church will soon leave this world in a cloud of glory. God is calling out a people for a prepared place and preparing a people to finish up His work in the Church of the Living God. She must be a glorious church, pure and white and clothed with the power of Almighty God, a pre-pared people, a peculiar nation, a called out nation from all the nations of the earth—a separate nation, a holy priesthood, children of the living God, God's sons and daughters. So now, the Lord is calling us to eat the strong meat, calling the saints of God to get deeper in God. They must be filled with the Holy Ghost, eat of the living bread. By continuing to eat we will never die spiritually. The time has come that we must have strong meat and we must receive it or be left behind in the Great Tribulation that is coming. One calamity after another is sweeping over the earth. Unless we get deep in God the waves and tribulations will sweep us away. Blessed is that servant, when Jesus comes to catch His bride away, that He shall find giving the saints of God their meat in due season. This Gospel of His kingdom must be preached to all nations, then shall the end come. This Gospel must be backed up by mighty signs and wonders, people filled with the Holy Ghost, baptized in the fire.

Won't Walk in the Light

People don't want to walk in the light; they don't like the way. They say, "We will be despised and they will call us all kinds of names." If they can call us any worse than they did the Son of God I'd like to know it. But if we suffer with Him we shall reign with Him. He has promised us everything in this life with persecutions. We all want the good things, but not the persecutions. They that will live godly shall suffer persecutions [2 Timothy 3:12]. Bless God, He is around us like a wall of fire. He that is in us and around us is more than he that is against us.

Will you belong to the royal line, accept the invitation, eat of the strong meat? Will you be baptized in the Holy Ghost? God help us to say yes. Will you go up on the mountain top and help make up the little flock who will fill the earth with a blaze of glory? For the wise, they that are deep, when Jesus comes shall shine as the sun. Those that are wise will put the sun in the shade. Don't you see how you can glorify God? He is coming in the glory of His Father, in the glory of all the angels, coming for His bride; and the saints that are alive in that day will be taken up alive. We shall not all sleep, but we shall all be changed [1 Corinthians 15:51]. Bless God! He makes our feet like hind's feet, makes us jump and dance with joy. It is the resurrection power.

But you say, O! I would not be a fool. But you are one already. I would rather be a fool for God than for the devil. To every one that is not saved He says, "Thou fool." I would rather be one of God's wise little ones if all the people in the world called me a fool. For the wisdom of this world is foolishness in the sight of God. The wisdom of this world shall perish. Men are trusting in their money and education and all those things in the place of trusting in the arm of the Almighty God. All these things shall perish. But look at the Great White Throne, see the River of Life, see the wonderful things God is preparing. The things we see here shall perish, but the things we see in the Spirit up in heaven, they will last forever. God will gather us up and take us where the people never get old! No death! No children crying for bread! No prairie fires! No wars! Bless God, we are going! Don't you want to join the procession? Don't you want to sell out? Leave the city of destruction and run from the storm; don't tarry in the plain. Prepare to meet God. Prepare for the coming of the Lord because He is coming. Let us not be foolish like the great company of those disciples who had the light. Some had been healed, many had been saved and come to know that God is good.

But people are saying today like they said then: "Have any of the priests believed? No, not many. Well, I guess I won't then." Priests will go to hell; ministers, too, if they don't get right with God. Priests and ministers all have to go the same way through the little gate, wash in the fountain and be made white to get eternal life. If you expect to go up you must tarry at your Jerusalem and be filled. In heaven they won't be mortal, nor in the grave, but the Holy Ghost will quicken the mortal bodies and like David you will say, "By thee I have run through a troop; and by my God have I leaped over a wall" (Psalm 18:29). Power to make you dance, get out of the mud and run up the mountains. Bless God! Let us get out of the mud and get cleaned up and dressed up for heaven. Join this race. God is filling the people. There are great degrees of glory, but every one can take another degree, and another, and another, and they won't have to pay a lot of money either—until you come into the perfect image of Jesus Christ. But you say, I don't want to give up this and I don't want to give up that. If you had any of the love of God in your heart you would not want to do these things, because you would be a new creature. Old things would pass away and everything would be new. But the trouble is you don't want to walk in the light.

Stubborn or Fearful of Being Laughed At

Many people see the light, but they are too stubborn to walk in it. You don't want to go that way, be laughed at and all that. Dear friends, what do you care. How many draw back through fear, fear of being laughed at, fear you will lose your position or be thrown out of the synagogue? Bless God, they cannot turn you out of heaven. God is pouring out His Spirit and many have had the real Pentecostal power, but they are not willing to acknowledge it—they are not willing to go forward and they begin to draw back, sinning against light. Refusing to walk in the light, they get leanness of soul. First thing you know if you fail to walk in the light you cease to have fellowship with Jesus, the blood ceases to cleanse, and you begin to invent excuses to ease your own guilty conscience. You were not willing to acknowledge you did not know it all. Behold, I show you a new thing—you did not know it yesterday. Behold, I show you new things from this day. Things you never knew before. So many of us do not want to acknowledge that we don't know it all. We don't know anything as we ought to and there is so much more for us. Let us cut the shore line and get where the Spirit lets us down into the deep things of God. So [some] people are not willing to walk in the light. Thousands of people that have come up against the Pentecostal Movement have declared it was the devil and all that and when we refuse to walk in the light it is death to our souls; especially if we lay hands on the ark. It is spiritual death to that man's soul if he does not make it right.

So there is great confusion, a great many just born being filled with God and being baptized in the Holy Ghost and God is revealing wonderful things to them and they are going on and on, thanking God for what they have and taking degrees in glory. Some are coming up through the press where everything is against them, all the devil's old rubbish—going up stream—but they will land on the mountain top when Jesus comes to catch His bride away. It is the sifting time. We find that when Jesus takes them away He will come back with those He takes away on white horses. This little flock! He is coming back! We are told that Jesus is coming on a great white horse with a great army from heaven behind Him, all on white horses. The bride of Christ shouting glory to Him that bought us with His own blood. He took them away from earth and took them home to heaven and made them kings and priests to God and they will reign one thousand years. And this little flock will be taken up very soon.

The time came at Pentecost when the few out of many thousands were willing to be called fanatics, and God, true to His promise, owned and accepted them with a cloudburst of glory and filled their bodies with the Holy Ghost. God spoke through them in other languages. They were ignorant, unlearned people, but God took possession and got hold of their tongue and spoke through them as He said, "With stammering lips and other tongues will I speak to these people," yet for all that some don't want to hear.[1] They could afford to be laughed at and brought to death to have such a visit from heaven and have God smile on them.

King's Daughters

He must become the fairest among ten thousand and the one altogether lovely and we must be willing to leave everything and every one on earth to follow Jesus. And the great holy Bridegroom is getting ready to come and take away His bride. Fear not little flock, it is your Father's good pleasure to give you the kingdom.

Are we going to backslide in the place of walking in the light? Are we going to eat the strong meat, or are we going to say the way is too hard and go off and grumble and growl and be lost forever? We are a royal line, King's daughters, a company of nobles, children of the living God that will go up—a great company. Every last one will be kings and priests. Bless God, we are going to ride on the white horses and come back to the great battle of Armageddon. But we must have the white robes on down here and follow the Lord wherever He goes. If you are persecuted for Christ's sake, great is your reward in heaven. But if you are persecuted because you walk crooked you ought to be persecuted enough to get down and get right. If you are wrong it will take persecution to get you right, but if you are a child of God and these persecutions come, then you can look up and rejoice because great is your reward in heaven.

Jesus is coming soon. He is giving you an invitation to the wedding. Will you accept it? Will you be one of the little flock? The angels are holding back the four winds—and they are crying, "Shall we let loose?" No, not until we have sealed the servants of God with the seal of the living God in the forehead. Perhaps you are a servant of God, you want to be sealed, be baptized in the flesh, filled with new life. And some of these days we will burst these bonds and go up to meet the Lord in the air. You that love Jesus will be tested. God is asking us that question: "Will you also go away?" Is the way too hard, is the price too great? Make up your mind you will stand on the rock and if the whole world should leave, you won't because Christ will be sufficient. We are going to be tested as never before. It is going to be harder every day, even among the people of God, because so many false teachers are coming in. It is a day of delusions—all kinds of delusions are coming. Keep under the blood, keep white, keep holy, keep pure and God will give us wisdom. Glory to God!

Chapter 10

The Great Revival
in Jerusalem

AND GREAT FEAR CAME UPON ALL THE CHURCH, AND UPON as many as heard these things. And by the hands of the apostles were many signs and wonders wrought among the people; (and they were all with one accord in Solomon's porch) (Acts 5:11-12).

This was the greatest revival given in the New Testament, greater in many ways than Pentecost. Then they were all with one accord in one place, awaiting the outpouring of the Spirit. They all made the same sound. You get there and God will shake the country.

Signs and wonders were wrought and of the rest durst no man join himself unto them. They were so full of fire no one dared to say falsely, "I am one of you." They were afraid God would strike them dead. God wants to get a people so full of power, His power, that others full of wildfire will not say, "God sent me."

What was the result? Believers were added to the church? No, to the Lord; multitudes both of men and women. Some say that this excitement, this fanaticism is good enough for women, but there was a multitude of strong minded men here.

They brought the sick into the street and laid them on beds and couches, that Peter's shadow might overshadow some of them. See what a cranky set they were! I wish we were just like that. Excitement rose higher and higher.

The whole country was stirred. There came a multitude out of the city about Jerusalem, bringing the sick, and they were healed, every one; healed because they came right. A wonderful revival, was it not?

In the midst of it, it was broken up. The high priest and Sadducees arrested them and put them in prison. Bless God, they did not stay there long. God sent His angel down and brought them out and told them to go into the temple and preach to the people.

It took some grace to do that, did it not? To go right back there and preach all the Word, not leaving out divine healing, but showing all the signs and wonders. In the morning they sent to bring them out. They found the prison locked, but no one there; those they sought were out preaching.

It is better to obey God. We are determined to obey God, let the result be what it may. God's people must meet persecution. People say this work is not of God. That is the kind of talk the devil likes to hear. All the devil has to do is to blow his whistle and his army runs to do his work.

One Shall Chase a Thousand

God has to blow and blow before He can get His people to do His work; yet we have the promise, "One shall chase a thousand." The devil hates holiness and power; he persecutes, and persecution is all that makes men fit for heaven.

This was a great revival. Every one of the apostles seemed to be there and God gave them wonderful power. Many mighty signs and miracles were done by them, because they were of one accord preaching and believing. Because of this, the fire of God fell upon the church and sinners began to tremble.

I believe in preaching in such a way that the power of God will make people tremble, preaching holiness, coming up to the front to do His will. "The fear of the Lord is the beginning of wisdom" (Psalm 111:10). The first we know of God, there is a holy awe comes over us. When we want God to work, to cause His presence to be felt in our midst, we must feel He has the power to work among His people; and it is a terrible thing to resist.

We must get on the full armor, and rush into the battle. "Press the battle to the gates" (Isaiah 28:6, author's paraphrase). Vain is the help of man. There is no shelter except in the wounded side of Jesus. It is the only place on earth to which we can flee. We learn there the way of righteousness, and we know what awaits the sinner if he does not accept this shelter.

God Confirms His Word

In the Old Testament we read of God's workings among His people. When some one was sent with a message, it often seemed very foolish, humanly speaking. What was the outcome? God always showed Himself and put His seal upon His work. When the message was delivered, He came forth with the supernatural, with the sign of His invisible presence.

He manifested His presence in miraculous ways. That put His fear upon the heathen. They said there is no God like the Hebrews', because of His wonderful works. He was a God to be feared.

In the New Testament, signs and wonders were done before the people. Wherever Jesus went the people followed Him. God was with Him, putting fear upon the people through miracles, signs and wonders, God wrought through Him.

He said, "I do not these things of myself. The Father, He doeth the works" (John 14:10, author's paraphrase). The apostles said the same: "By the mighty power of the Holy Ghost, Jesus doeth the works." Not I, but Christ. It is the same today.

In the signs and wonders today it is "Not I but Christ." He dwells in these bodies, and the work is done by the mighty power of the Holy Ghost. "Know ye not that your body is the temple of the Holy Ghost?" (1 Corinthians 6:19). Jesus Christ dwells in us. We are God's powerhouse.

It was by the hands of the apostles, not of angels, that God did His mighty works; and people believed when the signs followed. Jesus commanded the unclean spirits to come out and they had to come; the power of the Holy Spirit went through the apostles' hands and that is just the way God works today.

The apostles were not afraid of persecution, the sword, or anything else. They faced death in any form, rather than disgrace the cause of Christ by being cowards. It is a mighty God we serve, and today Jesus Christ who ascended into heaven is here by my side. He will lead His hosts on to victory. Let us press the battle to the gates.

This sect is always spoken against, misrepresented and lied about; but Jesus Christ is leading on His hosts. God permitted Jesus to be nailed to the cross and laid in the grave, but He came forth like the sun.

God permitted the apostles to be arrested, and put in prison; then He had an opportunity to show His power. He sent His angel and delivered them. The angel of the Lord is with His own. Our citizenship is in heaven. We are children of a King.

Around us day and night are ministering spirits sent to minister to those who are heirs of salvation. We can afford to be misrepresented, or even put in prison, if only we are looking for the manifestation and the glory of translation, to go sweeping through the gates.

Persecutions Come When God Works

The apostles were persecuted and the meeting broken up in Jerusalem, where the Lord was crucified. The meeting was held in Solomon's porch, one of the prominent places in the city. It seems the apostles were in this great porch, and they brought the sick into the street on beds and couches and every way and laid them all around sick, blind, and those vexed with unclean spirits; a great multitude.

What would the preachers think if we brought the sick around the church in this way? When they were preaching one of those fine sermons, firstly, secondly, thirdly, if someone dropped a sick person down in the midst, they would send for a policeman quickly; you know they would.

The paralytic did not break up the meeting when brought to Jesus and dropped down through the roof, when He was preaching. He is our example. He was glad to have something like that, because it gave Him a chance to show His power. He forgave him all his sins and then made him rise, take up his bed and walk.

The people began to shout, "Glory," the same way you do here; you cannot help it. If you have not done it you will. A consumptive woman was brought in here in her night robe. I did not care what she had on, she was healed. Hallelujah!

When the paralytic was healed, they gave glory to God. People say today, "You never heard such a cranky set." If they had only heard them then! We have something to make a fuss about. Dead people never make much noise, do they? There is not much noise in a graveyard.

Some people are frozen and have their feet in grave clothes. May God take off the grave clothes and set us free! David danced before the Lord with all his might. His wife did not like it, she thought he had disgraced her before the hand maidens and she began to grumble.

He said he was not dancing before the hand maidens but before the Lord. It is dangerous to lay your hand on the work of the Lord. She had no child to the day of her death. It was a great disappointment to the Jewish woman, as each one hoped to be the mother of the Lord.

Do not lay your hand upon the work of the Lord. It meant sudden death to lay your hand upon the ark of the Lord. Beware of sin against the Holy Ghost. That is the unpardonable sin and can not be forgiven. Sometimes the Holy Ghost comes like a mighty rushing wind from heaven, and makes a great commotion among the people; sometimes silently. He comes to us here.

You want to take down your umbrellas and get your buckets right side up. God will fill the vessels and make you a powerhouse for Him; then God will show himself mighty to pull down the strongholds of the devil and build up the kingdom of Christ.

You will have power to preach, and signs and wonders will be wrought as in the days of the apostles. The Lord was with them. He was invisible, but He was with them, confirming the Word with signs and wonders; and He will never forsake us if we obey Him.

Signs and wonders following. Following what? The preaching of the Word. He is here and ye shall see Him with what we call visible signs. Peter said, "This you see is the Holy Ghost." If you are willing, you will see it here, for God is coming in a wonderful way.

Fire on the Apostles' Heads

They saw the fire on the apostles' heads and heard them speak in other tongues as the Spirit gave them utterance; they saw them stagger like drunken men. Wherever the Holy Ghost is poured out you will see signs.

That was a great meeting, the sick were brought on beds and cots, and God, at the hands of the apostles, wrought many signs and wonders. The fear of God fell on the people. Thousands and thousands were converted to God.

Their names were written in heaven; they were filled with the Holy Ghost, the glory of God; the power of God was so great they could not get close enough to have hands laid on all the sick. Peter seemed to be the leader in this divine healing movement and they tried to get them near enough that Peter's shadow might overshadow some of them.

The power was of the Holy Ghost. He that believeth on Jesus Christ shall have such power that out of his inward parts shall flow rivers of living waters. The Holy Spirit is like a river. Pentecost filled the apostles, and people were healed even watching for Peter's shadow.

The power of the Holy Ghost struck the sick ones, and healed them and the people marveled. Jesus did many mighty works, and He told the apostles they should do greater things than these if they believed on Him.

Men and women, God wants you to get into that place. Don't you see God works through human instrumentality? God will use us if we are swallowed up in Him. In Chicago, people were healed sitting in their seats, and away up in the gallery some fell like dead people.

The power of God is going out while I am talking. You know I am speaking the truth; believe it, accept it and get more of Jesus. If we take in and take in, and do not give out, we are like a sponge which needs to be squeezed. Let us get so full that it will run right out through us; not absorb and absorb, and never give out.

Many of you are baptized with the Holy Ghost; you ought to send the power this way while I send it that way, and when the two come together something would happen. I could not keep my feet if you would do this, glory! Glory to God!

Take a picture of that revival. Did they act like crazy folks? Some of the best people in Jerusalem took part in that revival. All classes were there. People were lying all around, getting healed, or running to bring someone else to be healed, and multitudes were saved.

Healing the Sick Is Part of the Gospel

It was the greatest revival, divine healing was the drawing card. When people are healed, it does not mean simply healing, but it brings people to Christ. Take the man healed at the Beautiful Gate of the temple.

Peter took the miracle as his text and preached. The authorities laid hands on him and commanded him not to speak or teach in the name of Jesus, but Peter and John and the Holy Ghost came in great power. The outgrowth of that healing in the temple was a great revival.

Notice the mighty power that went from Peter's body. His very shadow healed people. Paul did special miracles; from his body were sent out handkerchiefs and aprons and the people were healed through them. This is different than any other miracle in the New Testament, but God is doing the same thing today.

The Holy Ghost works through our hands, through our bodies! We are sending out thousands of handkerchiefs all over the country; over land and sea. I could tell you wonderful stories of the work they do; five were healed from one handkerchief.

As we hold up Jesus, God sends His power through us, as He did in apostolic days. Let us arise and shine and give God the glory.

When I first started out to preach, I did not know I was to pray for any one to be healed, but God showed me I was to preach divine healing. The devil tried to keep me back, but thousands have been healed and saved through healing.

I lay on hands in the name of Jesus. 'Tis Jesus makes you whole. Sometimes the power is so great they are healed instantly, leaping and jumping and praising God. The Lord is here, we can have as great a revival as they had in Jerusalem, and the fear of God will be upon the people.

God wants you to march to the Cross and give glory to God. We want to get to work here. Let Him do the work in your soul first. We are going to have a revival here like the one in Jerusalem, with many signs and wonders.

Getting divine healing isn't like going to the doctor. Get baptized with the Holy Ghost before you leave; then when you get home you will not backslide. Glory to God!

Chapter 11

The Fire and
Glory of God
Filling the Temple

A SYMBOL OF THE OUTPOURING OF THE HOLY GHOST
ON THE DAY OF PENTECOST

Second Chronicles 5:11-14: And it came to pass, when the priests were come out of the holy place:

I want you to see how they came; 120 of them with different instruments, yet all making the same sound; the Levites arrayed in white linen, emblematic of purity.

It came even to pass, as the trumpeters and singers were as one, to make one sound to be heard in praising and thanking the Lord; and when they lifted up their voice with the trumpets and cymbals and instruments of musick, and praised the Lord" (2 Chronicles 5:13).

There were 120 priests blowing trumpets, there were singers and instruments of music, but they were as one, to make one sound.

For he is good; for his mercy endureth for ever: that then the house was filled with a cloud, even the house of the Lord; So that the priests could not stand to minister by reason of the cloud: for the glory of the Lord had filled the house of God (2 Chronicles 5:13-14).

The 120 priests who were supposed to minister, stood like statues, and the Holy Ghost took the meeting. The entire building was filled with the glory of God.

All this demonstration, the house filled with the glory of God, was brought about by the 120 priests blowing the trumpets; the sounding of the different instruments mingled with the voice of the great company of singers; the whole object being to glorify God, and all making one sound.

God wants perfect harmony. No one criticizing, no one finding fault, but all sounding forth His praise; and in white-purity. If we go out to meet God clothed in white, washed in the blood of the Lamb; if we go out, all making the same sound; if we go out to glorify God, God will honor all the noise.

It is not excitement. God comes down to acknowledge the praise. They pressed the button, and the power of God came down. That same power will either save or destroy us some day. The house was filled with the power and glory of the Lord.

Living Temples Praise God

There was no preaching then; but singing, shouting, praising the Lord, and all that praised, glorified God. The house was filled with His glory. The people were still standing, Solomon was ready to dedicate the temple; the temple represents the Church of Jesus; it also represents our bodies. "Know ye not your body is the temple of the living God?" [1]

Two or three verses from the seventh chapter of 2 Chronicles: It is like Pentecost; represents Pentecost. "When Solomon had made an end of praying" (2 Chronicles 7:1). So many people never look to God to answer; they would be frightened if He did. Solomon stretched out his hands and prayed to God, and God heard him.

When he had made an end of praying something happened. God will come forth if you are not afraid of the power, if you are ready to stand for God with all there is of you. As Pentecostal people we should always be "prayed up," so we can get hold of God quickly, and be sure it is for the glory of God.

"The fire came down from heaven, and consumed the burnt-offering and the sacrifices; and the glory of the Lord filled the house" (2 Chronicles 7:1). Some people talk as if God never had any glory, as though the glory of God was never seen at any time.

Paul said, "If the ministration of death, written and engraved in stone was glorious,...shall not the ministration of the spirit be more glorious?" (2 Corinthians 3:7-8; author's paraphrase).

The glory under the Law did not last; but the Holy Ghost came at Pentecost to stay, and the manifestations under the ministry of the Holy Ghost are to be with much greater glory, to "exceed in glory;" the power under the Law was only a shadow of what we ought to have under grace. This was the ministry of life, not death.

The house was filled with the glory of the Lord; they saw and felt it; it was not a shadow. I am glad the glory of God has been seen here a number of times. Many times in our ministry the glory of God has been seen over us. God is here. This you see and hear; "This is that"; this is the promise of the Father; this is the Holy Ghost.

The priests could not enter into the house; they could not get in at all, because the glory of the Lord had filled the Lord's house. "When all the children of Israel saw how the fire came down, and the glory of the Lord upon the house, they bowed themselves with their faces to the ground upon the pavement, and worshipped, and praised the Lord, saying, For he is good; for his mercy endureth for ever" (2 Chronicles 7:3).

Everything connected with this represents this glorious age. The apostle says God can reveal His doctrine which was hidden from all ages. Those who crucified the Lord did not know about the mystical Body of Christ. This divine life in us, they did not know it, or they would not have crucified Him.

It could be revealed only when the Holy Ghost came down from God to make men understand the New Covenant. The glory that belongs to the ministration of death did not come to stay. The glory came from the ark of the covenant, containing the tables of stone on which the Law was written, the Ten Commandments.

There were the cherubim, two angels, facing each other, with wings outspread over the ark and mercy seat, where God dwells in His temple. In His tabernacle nothing is supposed to be in the heart but God's Word, the new and everlasting covenant, written on the fleshy tables of the heart, not on stone, but with the finger of God Almighty.

We May Always Be Filled
With the Glory of God

If, when the people obeyed, the glory of God came down and the people fell prostrate, how much glory ought there to be today? There was just one tabernacle, and two tables of stone. Today your body is the temple of the living God. Our bodies are the temple of the Holy Ghost—and God with His own finger writes His Word in our hearts.

The ancient temple in all its glory represents each one of our bodies. If we are filled with the Holy Ghost, as we ought to be, the body will be flooded with rivers of water flowing out to others; and it will be on fire for God.

The glory of the Lord was seen over the ark; inside the tabernacle the lamp was always burning, being kept supplied with oil; it never went out. In the temple of the body God puts His love in our hearts, and He wants us to keep the light always burning; never to let it go out.

By keeping all obstructions out of the channel of faith, we get a supply of oil continually; and the light shall shine through the tabernacle always. If the oracle written on stone was glorious, how much more glorious under grace! The Holy Ghost shall abide with you always. Glory to Jesus!

Jesus said if we keep His commandments, the Father and He would both take up their abode with us. They dwell with us, and we are flooded with the Holy Ghost. [We are] people to be wondered at. "Here am I, and the children Thou hast given me" (See John 17). There should be perfect fellowship and harmony; we should all make one sound. The glory came down at Solomon's prayer. At a glimpse of that glory they lost their strength and the whole multitude went down.

When we are praying for people to get saved or healed, some shout, some praise, some pray, but all are making the same sound. We put on the blood by faith, and get a glimpse of His glory. Is it any wonder people lose their strength and fall prostrate under the new life which comes to them?

Is it strange we are people to be wondered at? You have seen all this here: singing, playing, making the same sound. Is it any wonder these people who come here, especially to get under the blood as never before, when they get a glimpse of Jesus, is it any wonder they fall prostrate?

You must prove God has changed, has taken His power away before you condemn us. His gifts and callings are "without repentance." He never changes; He is the same yesterday, today and forever.

No one has any right to condemn us, to say the people are hypnotized, crazy, have lost their minds, or I have put a spell on them. Great God! awaken the people before the thunders of judgment shall arouse them! You must throw the Bible away, or you must prove the gifts and callings have been taken from the church before you reject us.

We are going the Bible route, and you have no business to teach anything else; you must stick to the Word of God. We do not hold anything up but the Word of God. It is good enough for me. I am not ashamed of the Gospel of Christ, nor of His power.

What a wonderful people we are in our privileges! Today every one may be God's priest. If we abide in Him and His words abide in us, we may ask what we will and it shall be done. We indeed have wonderful privileges. The power of the Lord shines forth a hundred times greater than under the Law; the power then was typical of Pentecost.

Get your Bibles and search out these things; you are getting the light of God, and He expects you to walk in the light, even if you get it from the little weak woman. In His Name we tell you these things are true. What do you care for man's opinion when you stand before God? Dried opinions and traditions of men all go to destruction, but it is the living word that we are preaching to you.

John Gets a Sign

When John was in prison he began to doubt a little whether Jesus was the Christ, and he sent his disciples to ask, "Art Thou he that should come?" (Matthew 11:3). Jesus did not say, "I belong to the church or I belong to a college." He said, "Go and tell John the things you have seen here; the lame walk, the blind see, different diseases are healed, and the poor have the Gospel preached to them. Blessed is he whosoever shall not be offended" (Matthew 11:4-6, author's paraphrase). Men get mad at the signs of the Holy Ghost; jealous; spitting out hatred; trying to tear down God's work.

If John did not believe in Christ through the signs, no eloquence would be of value. If he did not believe what the witnesses tell him he would not believe anything; neither will you! There is a devil's counterfeit, and there is a genuine, as sure as you live.

If you only look on, it will seem foolishness to you as we praise God, and as people get filled with the Holy Ghost and get gifts; but it is Jesus first, last and all the time. We hold up Jesus and praise His Name. We see bright, happy faces; we see pain go out of bodies, and we go home rejoicing, feeling we have heaven here below.

Resist the devil in the name of the Lord. Sometimes when I am standing up preaching, the devil would make me drop dead, if I would listen to him. I resist in the Name of the Lord, and he has to go. We have such a wonderful Saviour!

You shall lay hands on the sick, it does not say where. He commissioned me and I obey God rather than man. Neither the deadly serpent or any poison shall harm you. Ye shall cast out devils; I believe every bit of it, and I have seen it all. Hallelujah!

I got my commission from the Lord, and I did not go until He called me; nor until I was baptized and qualified; I get my message from heaven. I do not know what I am going to talk about; but God knows everyone here, and just what every one needs, and He will give you something.

The power Jesus promised His disciples, when He told them to tarry at Jerusalem, was to change their lives and qualify them to transact the business of heaven. After they were baptized with the Holy Ghost they would be true to their Master and be witnesses for Him.

They went down from that mountain praising the Lord! They were filled with a great joy, as they went back to Jerusalem to await the fulfillment of the promise. They had confidence in God; He said so, and they began to praise.

Are you full of joy, having not a doubt about Jesus being your Lord and Saviour? You want power to do the work of God; you want to be clothed with power. God says He will baptize with fire, bestowing wisdom, knowledge and gifts. He will make you to understand the deep things of God, and as you teach them and live them, God will be with you.

Hearts Run Like Drops of Water

You must believe you are going to get this blessing. They were "with one accord." God help us to get to that place. God wants us of one accord; hearts running together like drops of water.

A little company like that could shake a city in a day. We are not of one accord when one is pulling one way, and one another; when we hear "maybe this," and "maybe that." Do you suppose God will bless you in that?

You can not understand the first principles. Once you have the new born joy in your heart, when you see it in some one else, you know it is of God. Be of one mind; no matter how much you have to praise God for, we always want more.

At Pentecost, suddenly they heard a sound like a mighty, rushing wind. This Holy Ghost we are holding up, is a mighty power; He came from heaven like a windstorm; like floods of water filling the vessels and as fire upon the heads of 120 people.

As it were cloven tongues of fire sat upon their heads; then the Holy Ghost went in and took possession of the temple; took full possession of the machinery, wound it up, and set it running for God. They staggered like drunken people and fell. This mighty power took possession of their tongues, and spoke through them in other languages.

It said away back in the prophets: "with men of stammering lips and another tongue will I speak to this people." Think of that! God doing such a mighty thing! But some do not want to believe. That is the way the Holy Ghost came, and comes today; and people say it is some other power.

They did not lose their mind; they had just found it! They got the spirit of love and a sound mind. We never have a sound mind until we get the mind of Christ. People who can not understand it, say these things are foolishness. We are told the wisdom of this world is foolishness with God. This is the power of God and this wisdom [is] of God, not the work of the devil; people saying so doesn't make it so.

God had complete control. He came in and took possession. The Holy Ghost is in the world today. You must prove he has been taken away, and also the gifts and callings, before you have a right to lay hands on God's people.

The things called foolishness today are the power of God unto salvation. Step out in the deep with God. Paul tells us the Lord ascended into heaven and sent down gifts, for the work of the ministry, the perfecting of the saints, the edifying of the Body of Christ.

God's Children Edified

The ministry does not want the gifts today. Saints, that is, Christians, are baptized with the Holy Ghost that the whole body may be edified; no matter how much you have got. When God is working, every one of his children is edified. If God works through some one else, I am edified and encouraged, and I rejoice.

The working of the Holy Ghost is the visible sign of the presence of Jesus. They went from Jerusalem to preach the Gospel everywhere, and the Lord was with them. I love that word. He is in heaven. Yes, but He is with us also.

The Lord was with them, confirming the Word. How? With signs and wonders following. Amen. Wherever they went they saw faces shine, some one healed, some one speaking in tongues. This you see and hear; it is the Holy Ghost, and it is for the work of the ministry.

If I did not know Jesus was by my side, and His loving arms around me, I could not stand here today. I should not have the strength if I did not know that He dwells in this body. If I did not know by experience that these things are true, I could not stand here.

I have tested the truth; I know it is of God. How can we help talking of the things we have seen? I have seen things by the Spirit, and in visions. I have seen Jesus; the heavens open; the marriage supper; hosts of angels; the glory of God. I have seen them, glory to God! I know what I am telling you. I know Jesus lives and is standing by my side, more truly than I know you are here. These things are verities.

I am not ashamed of the Gospel of Christ. Glory to God! When a weak woman comes here to tell you what strong men ought to have told you, what are you going to think about it? I say these things are true; and when people say they are foolishness and fanaticism, dare they attempt to prove it by the Word? I dare them to do it.

When they can prove the Holy Ghost has been taken out of the world, away from God's people, I am ready to go to prison, not before.

Chapter 12

The Former
and the Latter Rain

THE LORD IS IN OUR MIDST. BE STILL AND KNOW THE VOICE OF God. The Lord is in His Holy Temple; let all the earth keep silence before Him. Let us try to realize His wonderful presence. We must all meet Him sooner or later, as individuals; it is a good thing to get acquainted with Him now.

Acts 2:17-20. This Scripture applies to us today:

> It shall come to pass in the last days, saith God, I will pour out of my Spirit upon all flesh: and your sons and your daughters shall prophesy, and your young men shall see visions, and your old men shall dream dreams: And on my servants and on my handmaidens I will pour out in those days of my Spirit; and they shall prophesy:
>
> And I will shew wonders in heaven above, and signs in the earth beneath; blood, and fire, and vapour of smoke: The sun shall be turned into darkness, and the moon into blood, before that great and notable day of the Lord come.

This is a wonderful Scripture, and many do not understand it. There is a certain time spoken of here, when certain great and wonderful things shall take place, and people shall know that prophecy is being fulfilled. "It shall come to pass in the last days, I will pour out My Spirit," and there shall be signs in the heavens and on the earth—signs of His coming. The Holy Ghost will be poured out before the "notable Day of the Lord" comes.

This prophecy was first spoken eight hundred years before Jesus came to earth. Peter, standing up on the day of Pentecost, rehearses the prophecy and confirms it. Under the inspiration of the Holy Ghost, on fire with the Holy Ghost from head to foot, speaking with a tongue of fire, he said these things would come to pass in the last days.

We Are in the Last Days

We believe and know by the Word of God, and by the signs, that we are now living in the last days; the very times Peter spoke about when we were to know by the mighty things taking place. We are the people, and this is the time, just before the "notable Day of the Lord" bursts upon the world. We believe we are the people, yea we know it; we have a right to our belief, for it is based upon the Word of God, and no man or woman has any right to denounce our teaching, or to injure us in any way until it can be proved by the Word of God that the things we teach are not true.

You should give us a hearing; then take the same Word of God, and prove by it that the things we teach are not true—if you can. You must first prove that the Holy Ghost, working in all his mighty miraculous power, is done away with, before you have any right to denounce us as frauds and hypocrites, on account of these things, which we say come from God.

Whenever any one, minister or lawyer, can take the platform, and prove by the Word of God that the Holy Ghost and His mighty, miraculous power have been taken away from the church, we are willing to go to prison; not before. It can not be done. God never recalls His gifts; God never changes. My Bible says, "Jesus Christ the same yesterday, today and for ever" (Hebrews 13:8). There are many ways besides the working of the Holy Ghost, by which we know we are in the last days.

Joel in speaking of the last days, tells us many things we can not mention today, which show us that we are in this time. Nahum tells us when this time comes it will be the "day of his preparation" (Nahum 2:3), preparing men that they may be taken out of the world first, before the Tribulation comes.

Before the flood, Noah was commanded to build an ark. He was just five years building the ark—though many believe it was much longer than that—and the time he was building it was the preparation time in those days. Noah, at God's command, was preparing a place for himself and family, where they should be in safety, above the storm that was coming, above the waves and billows. At the same time the old world was getting a warning, Noah was building the ark.

Last Day Signs

Jesus compares that day of preparation to this time in these last days. It is a short period, and has been going on for some time. It is prophesied that there will be great signs in the earth, blood, fire, and smoke; earthquakes, great destruction; all these things have been coming upon the earth in the last few years. God has a time for everything. Daniel says, that in the time of the end, knowledge shall be increased, and many shall run to and fro; and Nahum says, "the chariots shall rage in the streets,... they shall seem like torches, they shall run like the lightnings" (Nahum 2:4).

Jesus sent the Holy Ghost with mighty signs and wonders. He took possession of men, and they staggered like drunken men; they were drunk, but not with wine. They spoke with "stammering lips and another tongue" (Isaiah 28:11). The things happened when Pentecost first came, to set up the church in power; that was the early rain.

In the last days, the time of preparation, God will cause to come again the early rain as at Pentecost, and He will also give the latter rain abundantly in the same month. What do you think of that? The early disciples went by the death route. It will take a double portion of the Spirit to fill our bodies, to make us sound in spirit, soul and body. When Jesus comes like a flash of lightning. He shall change these bodies of ours in a moment, and they shall be made like His glorious body.

"Behold, I shew you a mystery;...we shall all be changed" (1 Corinthians 15:51), and shall rise to meet the Lord in the air. When are these things to be? At the end of the day of preparation; just before the Tribulation bursts upon the world. We are to watch for the signs and not forsake the assembling of ourselves together; and so much the more as we see the day approaching! Glory to God! The Jews understood something of this. They say one to another we have been wounded, we have gone through many troubles; let us turn to the Lord. "After two days will he revive us: in the third day he will raise us up" (Hosea 6:2). The Holy Ghost was first poured out at Pentecost.

We are now down at the end of the second thousand years since Christ set up His kingdom. What about the Jews? The Jews today have great liberty in Palestine, so much so that they are going back by thousands and building up the waste places. Modern improvements are there today and they are hoping for something, they do not know what. After the Tribulation the Jews will return to the Lord.

"In the last days, saith God, I will pour out of my Spirit" (Acts 2:17); not sprinkle a few drops, but pour out on all flesh—a cloudburst! Just at the end; it will continue until the saints are taken away; then the Tribulation will burst upon the earth. Some of the signs will be, your sons and your daughters shall prophesy. It is very plain that every one may understand. There is to be a wonderful ministry in the last days. Paul says male and female are one in Christ. Both shall prophesy in the last days. That is the effect of the outpouring of the Holy Ghost. Other signs: devils shall be cast out, hands shall be laid on the sick and they shall recover; many shall speak with new tongues; if any one drinks poison accidentally, it shall not hurt him; serpents shall not be able to hurt in the last days.

The Bride Is Almost Ready

See the power given man today; he has even chained the lightning. It is the day for preparation. Men run to and fro and fly over the land. Hurry up! The ark will soon be finished, and then God will say, "Come up." The ark went up above the waters; the world went down. God is preparing His spiritual ark today; the body of Christ will soon be complete; and when it is complete it will go above the tree tops to meet our Lord and King in the air. We are in the day of preparation of the King of Glory, and His bride is making herself ready; rejoice and be glad, for the marriage of the Lamb is at hand. The bride must be arrayed in white linen, the robe of righteousness; clothed in the power of the mighty God, through His poured out Spirit.

She is getting her garments ready to meet the Bridegroom. I praise the Lord I am living in this day. The bride will be caught up just before the Tribulation bursts upon this sin-cursed earth. The bride must be very beautiful. She is represented as a queen dressed in a robe of finest needle work. What is that fine wedding dress, the garments, the bride will wear when she meets the Lord in the air? She will shine with the gifts and jewels of the Holy Ghost. We have this treasure in earthen vessels; but they that be wise shall shine as the brightness of the sun, and the wise shall know when these things are coming, when the ark is about ready to go up. The Lord will not keep any secrets from them, as there is perfect confidence between bride and Bridegroom, so Jesus will reveal secrets to His bride; He will show us the deep things of God, and we shall know when the end is drawing near. You must make your own wedding garments; you can not hire them made. The time is coming; people do not usually begin to make wedding garments until the wedding day is near. A bride is very happy, is willing to forsake her father's house, her friends, everything, and go with her bridegroom, even to a foreign country. She loves those she leaves, but he is dearer to her than anything else. We must be willing to leave anything and everything to go with Jesus. The bride will be taken out from among men, and men and women will be left. You may say, "I do not believe it." I BELIEVE IT!

Do you suppose I would leave home, friends, my only child, that I have, to spend my life for others, if I did not know these things were so? God has revealed these things by His word and by signs, and I know they are true. God is Almighty, is putting His seal upon this truth every day; He is putting the seal of the Holy Ghost upon people every day. The Holy Ghost is a witness to you, by mighty signs and wonders, that we are preaching the Word of God. I call God to witness that the Holy Ghost is putting His seal upon the work here. There are signs here every day. What are you going to do about it? If you believe the Bible, you must accept it. We have the Eternal Word to stand on, and stronger is He that is with us than all that can be against us.

Signs Follow the Word

After Pentecost, they went out and preached the Holy Ghost sent by the ascended Jesus; and He confirmed the Word with signs following. I say before God, He is confirming the Word here every day; and these miracles are put down in heaven's record. Jesus Christ is the healer and the baptizer. John the Baptist said, "He that cometh after me is mightier than I,... he shall baptize you with the Holy Ghost, and with fire" (Matthew 3:11), and I praise God that some of the fire has struck this place. You can make flowery speeches and the devil laughs; but this work stirs the devil. It is "By My Spirit," sayeth the Lord.

Paul said his teaching was not with enticing words of man's wisdom, but in demonstration of the Spirit and of power. That shakes the world; and it is just the same today. You say, I do not like this power; well, the devil does not like it either. I have been out in the world thirty-five years, and people fell under the power by thousands, before I preached healing. There were mighty outpourings of the Spirit that made the devil howl. It shows how little we know of the real Gospel when we take the letter of the law; it is like skimmed milk. No man can understand the deep things of God except by the Spirit. Paul had much knowledge; but He said the wisdom of this world was foolishness in the sight of God. True wisdom comes from heaven. The Word must be preached in simplicity. Jesus had the eloquence of high heaven at his command. Yet He used language that the most uneducated could understand.

Preach in a simple way, and demonstrate; the seal is put upon the Word by the Holy Spirit. Many say that when we lay hands upon the people they get mesmerized. I am sorry they do not know more of the power of God. There was a great revival at Samaria; Simon the sorcerer was baptized, but none of them had been baptized with the Holy Ghost. Peter and John went to Samaria, and laid their hands on them and they received the Holy Ghost. He was imparted to them in some way through the laying on of the apostles' hands. Simon recognized the power was different from sorcery, and he wanted it; he offered them money to give him this power that whomsoever he laid hands on they might receive the Holy Ghost.

The Gall of Bitterness

The apostles were horrified. They said, "Thy money perish with thee, because thou hast thought that the gift of God may be purchased with money" (Acts 8:20). The Holy Ghost and His power are gifts of God; you can not buy them. Many people today do not understand any more than Simon did. The apostles told him to repent or he would be lost. "Thou art in the gall of bitterness" (Acts 8:23). May God open the eyes of the people!

By the laying on of the apostles' hands something happened; the Holy Ghost fell on those people and they had great blessing. There were great demonstrations in those days when the Holy Spirit fell on the people. The thought is that when hands were laid on, something happened; they spoke in other languages, their mouths were filled with laughter and sometimes they fell like dead men.

You must prove that God has taken this power away before you judge us harshly. Peter said the things they saw on the Day of Pentecost were the things the prophets said should come. You ask why the people go down? What is our little strength under the power of God? Whenever people get a glimpse of God's glory, they lose their strength and fall. Paul said that in his vision he did not know whether he was in the body or out of the body, God knew. John the Revelator, when he saw the glory of God in a vision, fell as one dead. In Daniel's vision he fell upon his face; then a hand touched him and set him upon his knees and hands—you have never seen anything like that—then he was taken up, strengthened, and saw a great vision. The men that were with Daniel fled, so they did not see the vision, but Daniel fled not, and he saw it; but he fell prostrate. Just a little manifestation of God's power and we lose our strength and go down.

Some of you do not understand the working of the Spirit; you are not near enough to God to know it is the work of the Spirit. Peter was on the housetop praying; and he lost his strength and went down; a voice from heaven called him three times. Sometimes God teaches us more in ten minutes when we are lost to this world, than we would otherwise learn in months. Paul, as he journeyed to Damascus persecuting the Christians, was stricken to the earth when the light shone from heaven, and those who were with him also fell to the earth. Paul says the light was above the brightness of the sun; yet it was at midday when the sun was at its strength. All those men fell from their horses and rolled in the dust when the glory of God passed by. Paul was struck blind, and was blind three days.

When Jesus went to the grave, He went down a corpse, but when He arose from the dead, the soldiers were stricken down at the manifestation of God's power and glory. You must prove God no longer manifests His power and glory before you condemn us. Remember the first martyr, Stephen; he was a man full of faith, wisdom and power; full of the Holy Ghost. The wise men tried to confound him, but could not do it; then they were jealous and wanted to get rid of him. They hired men of the baser sort—that is the kind for that work—who lied about this mighty servant of God.

They arrested him, and there he was before the great assembly. He did not try to defend himself, but he took the opportunity offered to preach to them about Jesus. He was filled with the Holy Ghost; his face was as the face of an angel, and those who swore his life away saw it. He did not look like a liar and a hypocrite. He was a servant of the Almighty God.

You can see that light today sometimes in the faces of God's children. Stephen looked up into heaven, and saw the glory of God; he who had risen from the dead, standing at the right hand of ⅃ he told the people, "Oh, Lord, open the eyes of these people, ⸜ ⸝t them see the angels of the Lord encamped around about us and Jesus standing in the midst!" When Stephen told what he saw, they gnashed their teeth; they did not intend to repent; they dragged him out and stoned him to death; but the Lord received him and permitted it. God promises His people shall be protected and it is no sign He forsakes them because trouble comes. Stephen's enemies did not like it because God received him, nor did they like to see his face shine with the glory of God. His body was lying a bruised mass, but he rose to meet the Lord. He had a glorious vision. Do you believe he saw the throne, and Jesus standing there? People talk about these things as though they were fables.

Jewish Leaders Are Rebuked

God says before Jesus comes, these same "signs and wonders" shall come to pass; the sick shall be healed, devils cast out, people shall speak with tongues—just before He comes. I am so glad for these days. When Jesus came before, he rebuked the Jewish leaders. He told them they could discern the face of the sky, but not the signs of the times. "How is it ye did not look for me?" How much more shall He upbraid people when he returns? Why didn't you see the signs? Why didn't you listen to my messengers? Why didn't you look at the Word and see whether they were telling the truth or were impostors. Excuses won't do when we stand before Jesus. The light has come. Let us arise and shine, and give God the glory!

Nothing but the mighty Holy Ghost will ever take you up in the clouds; he will quicken these mortal bodies, and they will be changed. We shall not have wings, but our hands and feet will be made light. Our feet will be like "hind's feet," [to] run, skip and almost fly. We shall know the power of the resurrection life. We will be so filled with the Holy Ghost that our bodies will be made light. Sometimes my body is made so light, I can hardly stay.

My feet are on the earth, but my hands seem on the throne. Christ arose from the dead, and He is the resurrection and the life. People want to get the blood of Jesus over them, over their diseased bodies, in His Name.

Do you believe right now? If you believe to praise the Lord in faith it shall be done. If you do not feel the joy, offer praise as a sacrifice, and ask God to give you the joy. When the unclean spirit is driven out, the disease goes, and the resurrection life comes in; then you lose your little strength and go down like Daniel, John and the rest of them, and lie down in green pastures.

Some dance, shout and praise the Lord as the life of Jesus thrills through them. I declare to you on the authority of God and from my own experience, I know it is the power of God through Jesus Christ. It does not take Jesus long to do the work, but it takes some of us a long time to get there. Five minutes will do the work. Then the peace of God will flow through you like a river, and you will have joy in the Holy Ghost. As you go home, don't think about your sins; don't commit any more, and don't worry about the past, it is under the blood.

God gave me a message, and He has given me the strength to stand here and deliver it. He asks you in a loving way to meet the Lord in the air, to attend the marriage supper. Will you meet me there? He is coming so soon; I often think I shall live until He comes. I praise Him today, that I know these things. Sometimes people get into the flesh, and make too much demonstration, but that is better than never to talk, pray or sing; let us not condemn, but let us all try to get nearer to God, that is what I am striving for today. Oh, God, I have held up your Son today; I have honored His Name with all the strength you have given me. Take the scales off the eyes of those who do not see, and make them to see and make them to see the truths that have been brought out! May they think of them again and again and may they go unto You to find out whether these things are so.

You know how I have pleaded with people, not to lay hands on the ark, or on the Lord's anointed. Open the eyes of those who have only known dead forms, and make them to know I am Thy servant. Lord, I want the joy bells to ring in heaven because they are on the way, but you can not take them against their will. I pray I may meet them at the marriage supper of the Lamb.

Chapter 13

The Blood
and Fire Mark

EZEKIEL 9. THE VISION THAT GOD GAVE THE PROPHET nearly 2,700 years ago, and the same things are taking place today that took place at the time of the destruction of Jerusalem.

He cried also in mine ears with a loud voice, saying, Cause them that have charge over the city to draw near, even every man with his destroying weapon in his hand. And, behold, six men came from the way of the higher gate [men of authority], which lieth toward the north, and every man a slaughter weapon in his hand; and one man among them was clothed with linen, with a writer's ink-horn by his side: [Those with the writer's inkhorn represent the baptized saints before the destruction of Jerusalem, with the Holy Ghost in them, going around baptizing the people with blood and fire.] and they went in, and stood beside the brasen altar. And the glory of the God of Israel was gone up from the cherub, whereupon he was, to the threshold of the house. And he called to the man clothed with linen, which had the writer's inkhorn by his side [which represents the church today, the Holy Ghost working through us];

And the Lord said unto him, Go through the midst of the city, through the midst of Jerusalem, and set a mark upon the foreheads of the men that sigh and that cry for all the abominations that be done in the midst thereof. And to the others [the destroying army] he said in mine hearing, Go ye after him through the city, and smite: let not your eye spare, neither have ye pity: Slay utterly old and young, both maids, and little children, and women: but come not near any man upon whom is the mark; and begin at my sanctuary. Then they began at the ancient men which were before the house. And he said unto them, Defile the house, and fill the courts with the slain: go ye forth. And they went forth, and slew in the city. And it came to pass, while they were slaying them, and I was left, that I fell upon my face, and cried, and said, Ah Lord God! wilt thou destroy all the residue of Israel in thy pouring out of thy fury upon Jerusalem? Then said he unto me,

The iniquity of the house of Israel and Judah is exceeding great, and the land is full of blood, and the city full of perverseness: for they say, The Lord hath forsaken the earth, and the Lord seeth not.

[That is what they say today—the Lord doesn't see any more]. And as for me also, [He made me know that he lives], mine eye shall not spare, neither will I have pity, but I will recompense their way upon their head. And, behold, the man clothed with linen, which had the inkhorn by his side, reported the matter, saying, I have done as thou hast commanded me (Ezekiel 9).

The Lord said unto me—go through the midst of the city, through the midst of Jerusalem, and set a mark upon the foreheads of the men that sigh and cry for all the abominations that be done in the midst thereof and when it was done he came back and reported. It is done, I have finished, the last one is sealed, the door is closed.

The prophet had this vision nearly six hundred years before Jesus came; before the destruction of Jerusalem, and now it makes about 2,700 years since he saw that vision—that vision of Jerusalem; of the church; of the conditions of the world, especially the church. But we are living in a *parallel* time today in the world and the church and the same wonderful things are taking place today just before the Great Tribulation; just before the wrath of God is poured out without mercy on the people the same things are going on today. [I believe] the Lord showed the prophet the awful condition of the church and these things came upon the Jewish nation, but this time [they will come] upon the whole world.

The Jewish nation had sinned against God. They were God's peculiar people, God's called out people. He said, I did not call you out because you were the greatest, strongest, wealthiest, or best, but because you were the fewest. (God's chosen people have always been few.) But I have called you, chosen you, set my love upon you and from these people came the Law and the prophets and then came Christ.

God gave the Law from Mt. Sinai amidst mighty signs and wonders. And when the temple was dedicated, the presence of God was seen. God appeared, gave them priests and prophets and revelations from heaven. Spiritual signs, visions and angels appeared. God talked from heaven and did these things while his people obeyed; but by and by they got proud and haughty and lifted up and they began to glory in multiplying numbers; taking in people from other nations who were unsaved and whose hearts were not right with God and gave them high places in the church; gave them authority and power, gave them charge of God's holy vessels and they ruled the holy vessels with a rod of iron.

God warned them and warned them and finally began to show them that they had left the fountain head of living waters.

Broken Cisterns Won't Hold Water

But they hewed them out broken cisterns that would not hold water. They began to follow the wisdom of men. The glory of God appeared to [Ezekiel in chapter 8], picked him up by the hair of the head and carried him through space between heaven and earth and set him down at Jerusalem and told him to look and see the awful things—the holy places filled with pictures of serpents like devil worship today [Ezekiel 8:10]. Things that were unclean, showed him the abominations, took him into the holiest place, where he found twenty-five men sitting with their back to God and worshipping the sun and then [I believe] told him—"Now you go and take the pattern of the church in all its glory, when the glory of God filled the house. You warn these people and take the pattern of the glorious church and go and compare it with the pattern today and show them where they failed and see if they will repent."

He said they will never do it. But God does not say for us to run things to suit ourselves. They were warned. Son of Man I am sending you not among the heathen but among the people of Israel.

But they would not hear. They failed to know that the prophet of God was in their midst. So he stood and warned them, but it did not do any good and pretty soon the last prophet came and they rejected him. And the love and mercy and glory of God left them. And for nearly four hundred years, perhaps more, the children of Israel were left without holy priests, without prophets, without visions or revelations, except a few little ones, broken hearted little ones who were true to God.

They began to say, "Oh, God, how long, there is none that can tell us any more. We have no prophet, priests, visions, revelation, where are the signs?" All through the Word when people were right with God they saw signs of the invisible God. But when they backslid they lost the connection. The pipe got filled up, the flow of living water stopped;

they trusted in broken cisterns, man's wealth and knowledge, which is an abomination without God.

So that is the condition the Jews were in when Christ came; and, after they had been looking for Him for nearly four hundred years, they did not know Him. He said to them, "Why is it you do not discern the signs of the time. Your prophecy is fulfilled and you are living in the days when the Son of Man should come."

They had been saying, "God has forgotten; God doesn't see; God left the earth and the signs and wonders are all gone," and they began to follow men's wisdom; but they did not want the power of God. They left the fountain of living water. They did not want to hear a shout in the camp; did not want to see God's power.

But God is love. God does hear and God helps you to see that and when Jesus came he gave them another call just like the latter rain. He said the day would not come without a falling away. God knows how they fell away. God is visiting the earth again. Before Jesus came His coming was prophesied and when He came the Jewish nation had another chance—He offered them the kingdom. But they spurned Him and turned Him away and finally one day He wept over them bitterly and spread out His hands. Just what He is doing today. "Oh, Jerusalem! How often would I have gathered you from the destruction that is coming, now I leave you."

Blood Shall Flow Like Rivers

"This time your house [is] left unto you desolate; your city shall be destroyed; the enemy is coming; armies are coming in to lay your place desolate and blood shall flow like rivers."

But God warned His people. He had a people that had accepted Christ and they had followed the Lamb. They tarried at Jerusalem until baptized with the Holy Ghost and God revealed Himself to them and revealed the Word to them. He said, "One day," when speaking of the temple, "the day is coming when that beautiful temple will be destroyed; not one stone will be left on another and the city will be destroyed." The disciples said, "Lord tell us when that evil thing will happen, we want to know what will be the sign of Thy second coming and of the end of the world." So Jesus tells them and gives them signs how we will know today. Jesus is soon coming and the signs show He will come back soon.

We are concerned about the signs. They asked questions, they did not talk for foolishness and the Lord told them how they should know. He gave them signs and said when you see certain signs prepare to flee to the mountains. Make ready for the escape and then the other signs, and finally a certain sign. When you see this sign, if you have not made all preparations for flight; if you are on the house top, go not into the house; if you are in the field do not turn back to take your cloak, but flee to the mountains. Get out of the city because the gates will be closed and you will be shut in. They believed what God said; they took His Word by faith; they believed the Word, they felt the responsibility; they loved their people, and they knew unless they accepted Jesus Christ they would not escape. They were in the right, baptized saints sighing and crying because of their own people according to the flesh and their neighbors, sighing and crying on account of the awful things going on, but they were shut in with God. They had the mark of God upon them.

When you see the things that are making the world turn pale and tremble, lift up your heads and rejoice when this comes, rejoice at every calamity because it will soon be over. So, although they sighed and cried, still they rejoiced because they knew they were saved.

The Mark in the Forehead

The man with the inkhorn [in Ezekiel's prophecy] represents the Holy Ghost people. In a short time all these things are coming. Get busy, warn the people, whether they will bear or forbear, warn the people. We see the saints of God filled with the Holy Ghost. We see them go through the offices and stores and business places, and here are the people that are coming in this great army of destruction, going back and forth about their business, but the man with the inkhorn was to do the work, getting ready for the great work, but no one knew what was going on. And the saints of God are going everywhere warning the people the best they can. "Judgment is coming; destruction is coming; the city will be taken!"

They were laughed at as fools and fanatics and everything else. They would not listen. But the saints knew destruction was coming and the city would be taken; their business would be no good; the enemy would take everything. The only thing they could do was warn the people that destruction was coming. Their money and their homes, and silver, and land would not do any good. Neither will it do you any good. God helps you to see it and use your time and means to spread the Gospel. Blow the trumpet in Zion. Jerusalem will be taken; tribulation is coming; the time of the Lord is near, it hasteth greatly, it is even at the door. Warn the people that they must have the seal of God on their forehead. So we are going around getting the people saved, baptized with the Holy Ghost, and sealed with the finger of the living God in the forehead. They had to have a mark of God in the forehead to understand these things.

"Go through the city, cry and sigh, put the blood mark on them, and the fire mark on them, seal them with the finger of God."

And that is what God is doing today. Glory to God. That is what they did. The Word went out. They were laughed at, and scorned, and persecuted, and everything else; but they saw the signs coming faster, and the more they did the more they laughed at them and the more they persecuted them. They made huts away in the mountains and every day they felt worse about their friends and neighbors, and they would go to the city in haste and try to show the people these things were true. They did not believe. But that did not change the fact. This [was] the time of the great feast and the rabbis from all over the world were there. While they were gathered there the Lord had told them, "When you see a certain signal get out quick. Don't go back to take anything but get out of the city quick." The rest stayed in the city, they would not believe anything, they were having a good time. All at once the certain signal came, the gates were closed, they were shut in and they never got out. Those who had the seal of the living God upon them were caught up, taken out just like we will be only a different way.

Josephus, the historian, tells us that not one of the followers of Jesus Christ went down in the slaughter. They believed God and prepared for the escape, and God took every baptized saint. There was not one permitted to be locked up in that city because they believed God and made preparations for flight. Hallelujah.

We are a nation that are hated, a nation not desired, a nation despised. This sect is spoken against everywhere. I am glad I am one of them. When Jesus comes you will be willing to be called a Holy Roller or anything. God help you to see. They were all taken out. In Jerusalem they were all having a good time. The enemy came in and the gates were shut and the greatest calamity that the world ever heard of fell upon the Jews. The army went into the city and commenced at the court where the holy men sat; where twenty-five men were found with their backs to God worshipping the sun. They commenced at these fat priests and heads of the church and they were slaughtered first, like oxen.

[During the Old Testament seige of Jerusalem] we are told they had no provisions, did not expect anything, were shut in there and literally starved to death. Delicate women ate their own children. [Lamentations 4:10.] Delicate women who would not put their foot to the ground, ate their own children during the siege. Never such a thing happened before. You know all about those things. Some were carried away in captivity; only a few despised little ones left as slaves. But God's people had the mark—those who had sighed and cried—every last one was taken out. Oh, Hallelujah!

The prophet, Ezekiel, saw these things 2,700 years ago. He is looking down to us today. When Jesus comes there will be such a tribulation on the earth as was never known before. The darkness will be so great it can be felt. Such a time as the world never heard of when Jesus comes to catch His bride away. All that sigh and that cry for the abominable things that are going on in the world. Those who have the mark are the children. You will not be overtaken as a thief in the night for you shall know. The wise shall know. Glory to God. Oh, I praise God. Now then you see they escaped. They believed and obeyed. But those wise men, rich men and great men all went down in the slaughter. But those that were called fools; that were wanderers and pilgrims, who had to leave their homes and leave their wealth, they escaped with their life and a few little things they could take to provide for their comfort. When Jesus comes you won't take anything. All will be left for the devil to war over because the world is going on just like the Jews did. When Jesus comes it is not the end of the world but the saints will be taken out when Jesus comes.

Dear friends we are living in a time parallel to that. Jesus is coming again. God is visiting the earth again, pouring out His Spirit. The church has gone back. When I was a girl the Methodist Church was the most powerful and the most spiritual. They had an amen corner in every church and when the preacher would come in he would go right to the pulpit and commence. There were no secondlys nor thirdlys nor anything of that kind, they did not have time, and the amens came from all over the house. They obeyed God, and they were happy people, and they had great power.

But today [1918] they are saying, "We don't know God. He left us. We don't see Him. We don't like this way." So today there is not an amen nor a shout from anybody. And if one sister gets blessed and the power of God comes on her and she shouts, three or four good sisters get around and she won't shout the second time.

War, Famine and Pestilence

Lots of people are wrong today if those good old people were right. Dear friends, if they were right, then your own fathers, and mothers, and grandfathers, and you, would not like to have any one say they were crazy. If they were right before God some one is wrong today.

Now listen, God is pouring out His spirit again on all nations of the earth and today God has a baptized people; saints of every nation, church and tribe, are mixed up in this company, baptized in the Holy Ghost and fire who risk everything and warn the people. Get under the blood and get the mark of the living God in the forehead. God is visiting you again and we are just on the eve of the awful tribulations. Men and women will eat their own flesh. There will be war, famine and pestilence and all these things in one day. If you escape the war the wild beasts will get you. If you escape the lions and bears and stagger around in your own house for a quiet place to die a serpent will bite you.

Great God, don't you see these things are coming? Read the Word of God and watch the signs. These things were seen 2,700 years ago. A day with the Lord is only a little while and a thousand years only a day. We are the people on the stage of action today and the people who are living today will be in this great army of slaughter. But the saints will be taken out. Those living here tonight will never see death until they see the Son of God coming in glory.

So we see every day the signs being fulfilled everywhere that Jesus is coming. And that is why the saints today are making such an effort to go through the way, running the risk of everything to enlighten the people; to find hearts that will receive the message and get saved and let God seal them with the seal of the living God in their foreheads. Make the vision plain. God help me. Will the people [to] see that we are actors in this vision. Make it plain so that the one who hears may understand and when he receives the mark of God will run to get ready. That is what we are doing today.

Now beloved we must have this mark of God. Not only saved but sealed with the seal of the living God. It may be if you go deep enough that you will be hid away from all these things that are coming on the earth. Be shut in with God now today. The angels represented as holding back the four winds of the earth are letting loose now as sure as God lives. Another great angel cries, "Hold on a little longer." We wonder about these things. Angels see the awful condition of the earth; the cup of iniquity is full. O Lord can we let loose? Can the sun be turned on to scorch men; can the cyclones tear down the cedars; can the tidal waves sweep the towns away; can the earthquakes come? But the great angel who carries the Gospel of Jesus Christ says, hold on a little longer, hold on a little longer; don't let loose. Hold back the power of the sun; hold back the greatest tidal waves; the greatest cyclones; the greatest earthquakes and the greatest calamities until we have sealed the servants of God with the seal of God in the forehead.

You may be a servant of God, but you must be sealed with the seal of God—have the blood and fire mark—sealed with the seal of the living God. Hold back the great calamities—it would be a great inconvenience to my servants—they are the lights of the world—for the sake of the souls that want to be saved I will give my people a little more chance to work. Hold back, what for? Don't let loose. Hold back until we have sealed the saints of God with the seal of the living God in the forehead. My God, help these people to see—see why the sun did not get two or three degrees hotter and kill millions. Don't you see the signs of what is coming? One hundred fell in Chicago in the heat. A few more degrees and millions would have gone down.

Watch and pray. Be in an attitude of prayer or praise all the time that you may be counted worthy to escape these awful calamities and stand before the Son of God. Don't you see we have no time for telling what this or that one said. I am here to tell you what Jesus Christ said. I don't steal words from my neighbor—it is what Jesus said—it is "Thus sayeth the Lord."

In that day two will be sleeping in the same bed, one will be taken and the other left. Two will be working in the field, one will talk and talk all kinds of foolishness and you have to answer; suddenly there is no answer. You look up. Why, what is the matter, Tim? Where did he go? Yes—you find him if you can. He escaped before the gates were shut. Glory to God—caught away. That is just going to be the way it is when Jesus comes. He will take them up alive—they will be changed quicker than a wink—not another body, but this body will be so light—not waiting for wings, but we are looking for the dynamo from heaven to lighten these bodies. We will rise like He did—hands and feet like wings—we will go sailing through the air over the stars up to meet Him with a shout—Glory to God!

A Fountain of Tears

But with the people here it will be so different. Those that reject Christ will be left to go down. Oh, God, how we ought to be sighing and crying for the people that will be left—we don't sigh and cry enough. But at the same time we are so full of joy we have to give vent or explode. Be glad because you are living in the time of the latter rain, but at the same time we are sighing and crying because of the corruption.

Several times I have cried out—the Holy Ghost within me cries out and it came to me like the prophet said when he was speaking of this day. Oh, my bowels—my bowels! His body seemed to be bursting and his head was a fountain of tears for the destruction that is coming on the earth. Jesus is weeping over Jerusalem and how the Holy Ghost weeps through me, it seems as though I would cry until I would die, but I try to go on. God is putting a mark on those that sigh and cry for all the abominable things that are coming on the earth.

Dear friends, don't you see [that] the angels want to let loose the four winds. Oh, can we let loose—they are so wicked—let the people go. No, not until we have sealed the servants of God with the seal of the living God in the forehead. Go through the streets and put a mark upon every one that sighs and cries—put the mark of God on. Tell them to be baptized with the Holy Ghost. Jesus Christ will baptize you with the Holy Ghost and fire. He will give us wisdom—the mind of Christ—seal us with knowledge and we will not be left in the dark, but we shall be children of light.

You say you are saved and living pure and holy lives, but if you don't get this baptism and get the everlasting arms of Jesus around you, you will be carried away in the press and you will not be ready to go up when Jesus comes. But hold back until the servants of God get the light and until they are sealed with the seal of the living God in their forehead. There is not much time. The Lord is holding back these things. Are we about our Master's business? No wonder I don't rest. Trusting to God to carry me through. I know these things are true. God help us, we are getting pretty near shut in now. So many false doctrines of the devil coming, people going over to delusions. You must be kept under the blood or you will be carried away.

I praise God for the knowledge that Jesus is coming soon. Praise His Name forever. These awful things are already on the earth. You know the Lord said when certain things happen it is the beginning of sorrows. The nations are mad. Aren't they mad now—they are crazy. What are they fighting for—jealous hatred. One nation against another, several have gone down—look at them. No one knows the real truth. May God help you to hear. This is the beginning of sorrow. The four winds are going to be let loose as sure as you live. If all this is the beginning of sorrows, what will the end be? You may escape the worse things and be hid away.

The prophet looking down to the last days saw the saints going up. He says, "Come up, my people, and enter into the place prepared for you and shut the doors about you and hide you for a little while, for the Lord cometh down to punish the inhabitants of the earth and their blood shall flow like dust and their flesh like dung and they will not be buried" [Isaiah 26:20,21; author's paraphrase]. And in the European war tens of thousands have been burned—you know these things—nobody knows where they are. Isn't that being fulfilled now? If this is only the beginning of sorrows, what is the end to be? God is holding back the worst things. Europe has had the call. They have been warned and warned.

God gave a wonderful vision to a man that was raised for a Catholic priest. Two angels visited him in the night, made him to stand before a great congregation, and warn them of these awful calamities—told two thousand people how Europe had been warned, but they turned their back and rejected him and now he is warning them at the mouth of the cannon.

This country is the same way. God is giving them the Last Call— the last chance to be sealed with the seal of the living God, but they turn Him away. The last one will soon be sealed. God will call at the mouth of the cannon. This country will be bathed in blood after a while. The best thing is to hide away. God help us to be up and doing, to be clothed in white linen which is the righteousness of the saints— with the writer's ink horn which is the Holy Ghost through us calling the people to get right with God. Ask God for knowledge and wisdom and get the resurrection power in [your] body and when Jesus comes be snatched out of this world. We who are alive will not prevent those that are asleep, but the dead in Christ will rise first and shake off the dust and worms like dew and will go up with a shout.

Praise the Lord! They will be ahead of us. Don't be afraid about the dead who died in Christ, for when Jesus comes God will bring the dead with him—so God is getting in honor of His Son's wedding to meet the bride and the dead saints will be caught up first and they will come with God the Father when Christ comes to catch His bride away. We do not need to worry about the dead ones. They will come up. But the time is near. It won't be very long until we who are alive will meet them in the air. I will meet my husband who died two years ago. He said, "I am not looking to the grave at all." But his body is there and different saints in visions have seen Him go up in His glorified body and He will be one of the first to meet me when I rise in the air. Many dear saints have died shouting and gone to glory. They will be raised and I will meet them. All our dear friends that have died in Christ will be raised first. We will rise in our glorified bodies to meet the Lord in the air.

Now, beloved, don't let this message run off; let it burn in your heart because it is a message from the Lord—hallelujah. Something you have never heard before, but you hear it now. You see the parallel, the picture—don't you see it? Oh, believe it, you are being warned. Take your Bible, ask God about these people up here that you think are so light headed. I am glad I am light headed enough to believe God. I am glad I am getting light enough to go up in the air when He comes. Hallelujah! Glory! Some of the resurrection power! Praise the Lord! I am looking forward to going up in the sky—up in the air—not to the grave. Glory to God! Hallelujah!

Chapter 14

The Seal of God
on His People

GATHER YOURSELVES TOGETHER, YEA, GATHER together, O nation not desired;

Before the decree bring forth, before the day pass as the chaff, before the fierce anger of the Lord come upon you, before the day of the Lord's anger come upon you.

Seek ye the Lord, all ye meek of the earth, which have wrought his judgment; seek righteousness, seek meekness: it may be ye shall be hid in the day of the Lord's anger (Zephaniah 2:1-3).

This call is not to sinners, but to God's servants, to His children to eat the strong meat. Ye meek of the earth who have wrought His judgments.

You see you are saved, and are working some for the Lord, but He calls you to seek the Lord in a different way, and for a different meekness. He cries to you three times to seek the Lord, to seek meekness, and to seek righteousness.

He is giving you the call to the marriage supper, calling you to get oil in your vessels; to get baptized with the Holy Ghost; to be sealed with the seal of the living God, in the forehead, which is the seal of promise.

The Holy Ghost will also witness through you in other tongues, for you may have any of the gifts.

You shall have power after the Holy Ghost has come in as a witness.

The prophet has come warning you to escape the awful judgments that are now coming on the earth. It may be that you may be hid in the Day of the Lord's anger.

This is the only hope for you, and to escape the awful destruction that is about to sweep over the world, there is no other hiding place, no safety in the world. Oh! that you may be hid in the Day of His wrath.

Yes, you may be, but it depends on how far and how deep you get hid away in God's love and power and will, whether you will be hid in that day. You may be hid. He shows that His judgments will burst on the earth like a whirlwind, and that the wicked will be like chaff.

Dear reader, there is no doubt according to God's Word and the signs all around us, and the revelations, and warnings the Lord is now giving us through His Spirit, that this is the time, and we are the people, and we have no time to lose, for behold He cometh, and is even now at the door.

The text implies haste, Awake, Arise, Rouse yourselves. Flee to Christ. Get oil in your vessels.

SHOUT the cry, "Behold the Bridegroom cometh." Trim your lamps. Get sealed with wisdom, that we may be among the wise to sit with Christ on His Throne to judge the nations. Gather yourselves together. Yea, gather together. Oh, nation not desired. No one wants this people, that have come out of darkness into this marvelous light. This peculiar people, who appear foolish on account of the supernatural power, and visible works of the Spirit.

We are hated, and despised, and forsaken. Our name cast out as evil, misrepresented, and counted as the offscourings of the earth, but we are very much beloved in heaven.

When the prophet Daniel was asking God to explain these things that we now see, Jesus appeared to him, and sent the angel to him, to make plain the vision. The angel said, "O Daniel, a man greatly beloved" (Daniel 10:11). Understand the vision, and the words. Then again, "O man greatly beloved, fear not: peace be unto thee" (Daniel 10:19).

The Sound of the Bugle Call

We are the people that the Lord was showing him. Now the same loving words of cheer come to us through His Spirit, to "the Little Flock." The bride that is making herself ready. "To him that overcometh will I grant to sit with me in my throne" (Revelation 3:21). "Fear not, for I am with you, you are much beloved" (Daniel 10:11, 19; author's paraphrase).

The Lord is sounding the bugle call in a most wonderful way through some by the Holy Ghost. It sounds like the judgment day was here. It makes the people tremble. He is calling His saints together, to see eye to eye when He shall bring us to the heavenly Zion. Blow ye the trumpet in Zion. Sound an alarm in the Holy Mount, among the saints. Let all the people tremble. Go gather My saints together, who have made a covenant with Me by sacrifice. God help us to make the right kind of sacrifice. Oh, praise the Lord, that is my calling today, to get the saints together in one Spirit, one faith, and one mind: filled with love and oneness in Christ. Lost and swallowed up in Him and in His love and power.

In the preceding chapter He shows us the awful trials and the time of the Great Tribulation. From the fourteenth verse to the last of the chapter.

> The great day of the Lord is near, it is near, and hasteth greatly, even the voice of the day of the Lord: the mighty man shall cry there bitterly.
>
> That day is a day of wrath, a day of trouble and distress, a day of wasteness and desolation, a day of darkness and gloominess, a day of clouds and thick darkness, A day of the trumpet and alarm against the fenced cities, and against the high towers. And I will bring distress upon men, that they shall walk like blind men, because they have sinned against the Lord: and their blood shall be poured out as dust, and their flesh as the dung.
>
> Neither their silver nor their gold shall be able to deliver them in the day of the Lord's wrath; but the whole land shall be devoured by the fire of his jealousy: for he shall make even a speedy riddance of all them that dwell in the land (Zephaniah 1:14-18).

"After giving [you] this fearful warning, gather yourselves together, O gather together, that you may be hid in the day of His wrath" (See Zephaniah 2:1-3; author's paraphrase).

We are a nation among the nations:

> Ye are a chosen generation, a royal priesthood, an holy nation, a peculiar people; that ye should shew forth the praises of him who hath called you out of darkness into his marvellous light (1 Peter 2:9).

We are called out in this generation. We are a holy nation, a nation of kings and priests, called out from among men. We are royal because we are children of a king; a holy priesthood, heirs to a throne.

> Unto him that loved us, and washed us from our sins in his own blood,

And hath made us kings and priests unto God and his Father; to him be glory and dominion for ever and ever. Amen (Revelation 1:5-6).

Thou wast slain, and hast redeemed us to God by thy blood out of every kindred, and tongue, and people, and nation;

And hast made us unto our God kings and priests: and we shall reign on the earth (Revelation 5:9-10).

This shouting was going on in heaven, after Jesus had taken His bride up to heaven.

They had been counted worthy to be hidden away in the City of Gold, the prepared place, that Jesus had promised. The great marriage had taken place. The long waiting bride was made the Lamb's wife. They were all enjoying the great marriage supper of the Lamb. They were receiving their crowns and position in glory. Taking their thrones, and exalted stations, that their diplomas call for, that they had gained down here in the Holy Ghost School. Hear the shouting, they make the heavens ring, amidst all the brightness and glory of heaven. Oh, the meeting of the loved ones to never part. They are safe, safe home at last.

Jesus is the attraction, He is the One, all eyes are on Him, all are trying to get nearest Him, and give Him all honor and glory, for through His blood and power they have entered into His glory. He hath made us kings and priests to God and we shall reign on the earth a thousand years.

Yes, they were safe in heaven while the dreadful work of destruction was going on in the earth. They knew they were coming back to earth to rule with kingly authority to bless the people with priestly power. The saints shall judge the world. They were rejoicing because they were coming back to earth.

Chapter 15

Some Shall Not Taste Death: The Rapture and Binding of Satan

VERILY I SAY UNTO YOU, THERE BE SOME STANDING HERE, which shall not taste of death, till they see the Son of man coming in his kingdom. And after six days Jesus taketh Peter, James, and John his brother, and bringeth them up into an high mountain apart,

And was transfigured before them: and his face did shine as the sun, and his raiment was white as the light (Matthew 16:28-17:2).

For He was the Son of Man and He was the Son of God. He "shall come in the glory of his Father with his angels; and then he shall reward every man according to his works" (Matthew 16:27), according to the deeds done while in the body.

"Verily I say unto you, There be some standing here, which shall not taste of death, till they see the Son of man coming in his kingdom. And after six days"—literal days—"Jesus taketh Peter, James, and John his brother, and bringeth them up into an high mountain apart, And was transfigured before them: and his face did shine as the sun, and his raiment was white as the light. And, behold, there appeared unto them Moses and Elias talking with him. Then answered Peter, and said unto Jesus, Lord, it is good for us to be here" (but he did not know what he was talking about) "if thou wilt, let us make here three tabernacles; one for thee, and one for Moses, and one for Elias." But God settled the question. "While he yet spake, behold, a bright cloud overshadowed them: and behold a voice out of the cloud"—another person called attention—which said, "This is my beloved Son, in whom I am well pleased; hear ye him" (Matthew 16:28-17:5). Glory to God! Hallelujah! Glory to Jesus!

There is a great deal in this lesson. It shows both the kingdom of Christ which is very near at hand now and the translation of the saints, and it shows the Tribulation that is coming on the earth. And it shows the close of the Tribulation when Christ comes back with His saints, binds the devil, destroys the antichrist and His army and sets up the glorious Millennium.

Six days—the Lord was speaking to the apostles and He meant six natural, literal days, for just six days after they saw what He said they should see. But it applies to us—a day for a year and a day with the Lord is a thousand years, and it was four days before Christ came—four thousand years—and the two last days brings us down to today and makes six thousand years. So we are on the stage of action today, right at the close of the last day. On the sixth day close to the seventh day we will be ushered into the great Millennium—the thousand years of rest—the Sabbath day. Jesus speaks to us with as much force tonight and He applies it to us as He did to them.

A Display of Heavenly Glory

Only a little while, six days I say to you, some of you who are standing here shall never taste of death until you see my coming kingdom, for I shall come in all the glory of my Father's kingdom, with all the holy angels, and I shall come in my own kingly glory. I will give you a display of this glory in a few days—you shall never taste of death until you see this thing. They did not understand. Six days after that it came to pass. He took Peter, James and John, those who seemed to be always nearest the Master—more anxious to stand by Him than the rest, and they were initiated into a good many things the rest did not know. He took these three and slipped away from the rest and took them up into the mountain. Six natural days from the time He said—some of you shall not taste of death until you see this glory—I am going to reveal it to you. Hallelujah to Jesus! Let us think about it. The prophecies are fulfilled and it will be just a very short time now according to God's Word. I say to you tonight, this applies to us. I am coming in My kingdom in all the glory of the eternal world to catch my bride away. Some of you will never taste of death until you see this and take part in it. Glory to God! Hallelujah!

God Turns to His People Again

Those prophecies point to this time—this is the end of the Gentile age—the Gentile age is to wind up at the close of the sixth day. The Jews are saying, Come, let us return to the Lord, for we have been wounded and bruised—and He will heal us up, and the second day He will revive us and early in the morning of the third day He will raise us up. This is the second day. The Jews are being wonderfully revived all over the land—they never had such notoriety. They are reviving, their bands are being broken. But early in the morning it will only be a few days—Bless God!—He will raise us up. And He will raise them up from the grave and wonderful things are going to take place. Before the Great Tribulation the saints will be taken up—Jesus Christ shall stand up for His people and there will be such a time of trouble on the earth as the world never knew and never will know again— when the dead in Christ shall rise and the saints shall be taken up. So we are coming into the time when these prophecies are coming on the earth—the beginning of sorrows—and if this is only the beginning what will the end be? This is the preparation time when He will scatter the power of the holy people all over the world as a witness. God shall rise up in His power and majesty and God shall work His strange work by the Holy Ghost through His saints. Natural men do not understand.

Jesus is coming in His kingdom. Get out of the city of destruction, run up on the mountain—Bless God. Be ready for the manifestations of the sons of God. This is the preparation time. The last message—this Gospel of my kingdom shall be preached in the last days of my preparation for a witness to all the world—to every nation—not to every person. Then shall the end be. Christ will come and take a prepared people out for Himself—a people for His bride, and then the awful darkness will cover the earth; the Tribulation time will set in—the time of trouble will continue until the Battle of Armageddon when the antichrist shall be destroyed and two-thirds of all the earth will go down in war, famine, [and] pestilences and be devoured by wild beasts. But one-third will withstand the antichrist and escape all the troubles and calamities that come on this earth— [they will] go through the fire, persecution, famine, and when Jesus comes back to bind the devil and cast him into the pit, one-third of the earth will run out to meet Him and acknowledge Him as their Lord of Lords and He will call them His people and forgive their sins and they will call Him their God and they will be restored at Jerusalem. God has said it. For He says after He takes His bride away at the end of this tribulation He shall return with His bride riding on the white horse of power and He will come back to build up the waste places of Jerusalem—that the residue of men might seek after the Lord and all the Gentiles that have called on His name will be in that company of the one-third that won't go down in the tribulations. He is coming back with the saints at the end of the Tribulation to destroy the antichrist and the blood will be up to the horses' bridles.

There will soon be three suppers—the supper in the skies at the marriage of the Lamb.

The prophet John saw a great angel standing in the sun calling with a loud voice to the fowls of the air: Come gather yourselves together for the great supper of the great God, that you may eat the flesh of the kings and of the mighty men of the earth and those that sat upon horses and eat the flesh of the horses and drink their blood at the supper of the great God. The antichrist and his army will be destroyed when God will call the wild beasts and the fowls of the air to eat their carcasses, at the time when Jesus will come back and bind the devil and cast him into the pit one thousand years. But the one-third that have gone through everything and by the hand of God escaped will come out to meet the Lord with gladness, and He will accept them and forgive them and He will call them His people and they shall be established and the glorious Millennium will be ushered in. But before this the saints of God will be caught away. He is coming to take His people out and every one that is not ready to go up will be left behind and go down when the antichrist comes forth.

The time of the awful Tribulation is near. May the Lord help us to understand this, dear friends. The enemies of the Lord today are getting worse and worse—the cup of iniquity is full—the harvest of the earth is ripe and ready to be cut down and cast into the wine press of the wrath of God Almighty. So God is pouring out His Spirit. Glory hallelujah! Causing signs and wonders through the holy vessels which shall be as clay to scatter the power of God through the land. And the great angels are saying, "Cannot we loose?" When will all these wonders cease? These great [modern] inventions [of our day] are coming up in the preparation time. Not because they are, but because it is God's time of preparation. There is no end to inventions.

God's Day of Preparation

I will rise up and work my strange works in the day of preparation. Therefore be ye not mockers. Behold, I have the message from the Lord—the decree has gone forth and I will make a speedy riddance of all the mockers on the face of the earth. They don't laugh at a cyclone—they don't laugh at a great fire, but they will laugh and mock at God's strange work. Be ye not mockers, for I got the message from the Lord. It came from heaven and the decree has already gone forth. God will make a speedy riddance of all the mockers on the face of the earth.

This is God's work. He is giving the people a warning, pouring out His Spirit upon the earth for the last time to warn the people just before the notable Day of the Lord comes. Every nation will be warned through the mighty display of God's power. Repent and turn to the Lord and you shall be saved—the visible signs that God is here, the visible manifestations that this is God's message—the last message and that God through His people is scattering the Holy Ghost. We haven't a dead God or a dead Christ, but He ever liveth and He is right here tonight. God is scattering power over the land and warning the people against the things that are coming. And every one that has the mark of fire and blood will be taken out alive. Every last one. And then the antichrist will come forth—the man of sin—the awful antichrist— he will come forth in his awful power after the hinderers are taken out. Who are the hinderers? The Body of Christ.

Ye are the light of the world. And He shines in the heart just as He shines through the faces of the saints. Glory to God!

So God is warning you through His saints and getting people ready, sending out the warning in every direction to escape from the city of destruction and don't tarry in the plains. Get on your wedding garments, accept the invitation and get ready to take the flight through the air. When the saints are taken out there will be no restraining power—the devil will be let loose. People will sigh for one of these days—sigh and cry—there is no prophet any more, no priests. We don't hear from heaven—no light, all darkness—when the Holy Ghost goes up with the Body of Christ in the bride.

There will be awful darkness and the door will be shut and no one will have an opportunity to join the bride. The bride is being made up now. May God help us to see this. So the message is for you. Some of you here tonight will never taste death until you see the Son of Man. Never until you see the Son of Man coming in the clouds of heaven. Hallelujah! Keep looking up. Are you ready to go? If you are not, come tonight.

After six days, the disciples did not understand this, but He took those who were nearest, watching and praying and looking for those things to come true, took three of them and slipped away from everybody—nobody knew where He was—and He took them up into a high mountain (and that is a good place to be—way up above the world with the devil under your feet). How beautiful on the mountain are the feet of those who are running up and hurling back the glad tidings that Jesus is coming. That is a good place to go to pray if you pray right. Bless the Lord, it is not the long prayer or the loud prayer, but hallelujah! the prayer of faith. They were praying and something happened. He said, I am coming in all my Father's glory and in all the glory of the holy angels and some of you here are going to see this.

Peter, just before he went away, said, There will be lying wolves, but don't forget what you have heard. I have been telling you that He is coming again and I have not been telling you cunningly devised fables, but I am telling you the truth. I saw the king transfigured and I heard the voice of the great God of heaven. He came down to welcome the bride—He came down to be at the wedding—the cloud of glory settled over us and out of that cloud a great voice, the voice of God Almighty, and He introduced the bride to His Son. This is my Son, He is my Son, He is King of Glory. I am pleased at the selection of His bride. Hallelujah!

In the Twinkling of an Eye

They saw the manifestations. They saw Him just exactly as it is going to be when the saints go up. They had the picture—the vision. Fear not, little flock. In that vision he brought before their eyes the saints that are going up some of these days. There are some living here that will never taste of death until they see Jesus come. He brought the picture before them in a vision. Every tribe, tongue and nation on earth will be in that company, witnesses out of every nation. These three disciples were permitted to see them all changed just like they will be when He comes. We shall be all changed, we will not all sleep, but we shall be changed in a moment in the twinkling of an eye. We will have a glorious body like the Son of God and we shall be like Him, for we shall see Him as He is.

Now, then, John saw this picture twice. God has not left us in the dark. John was a man like we are, but God reveals the deep things of God to His saints. John had been banished to the Isle of Patmos. One time when he was talking to the Lord, behold the Spirit of God was all over and around him and he saw an open door and in a minute he was translated to heaven. He saw the saints go up and he went up with them. He saw thrones and those that sat upon them and he saw Christ on the throne of His Father. To him that overcometh I will grant to sit with Me on My throne, even as I have overcome and am sat down with My Father on His throne. He overcame the devil at the very last, and we must not only commence, but go to the end. When He overcame the last He went up and God gave Him a seat at His right hand—the highest place in the courts of glory—and He is there today. Stephen saw the glory of God and saw Jesus sitting at the right hand of God in majesty on high.

To him that overcometh will I grant to sit with Me on My throne as I overcame and am sat down with My Father on His throne. He has not taken His throne yet. John saw the saints go up the second time— then he saw Jesus take His throne and went up to the marriage supper. Blessed and holy are they that are called to the marriage supper of the Lamb. Blessed are they that shall eat bread at that supper and drink wine in my Father's kingdom. We are going to be substantial people, aren't we? Glory to God! Sit down to the marriage supper of the Lamb. That is the place He is preparing for you. O glory to God! Don't you want to be there?

We are a nation despised and hated—a nation not desired. The devil hates us and all his imps hate us, but He says, "Come, hide you away, come together—bind yourselves together and get ready for the manifestations of the sons of God. Fear not, it is your Father's good will to give you the kingdom." He will make us kings and priests in the sight of our God. Kings and priests, glory to God! So Jesus comes out and takes the throne and the bridal company will be the highest in heaven. There are great degrees of glory, but the overcomers—the bridal party will sit with Jesus Christ the Lamb of God on His great white throne through all the ages. They will follow the Lamb whithersoever He goes. They are the class that Daniel saw. They that turn many to righteousness shall shine as the sun. There are degrees to glory. I would rather be one of the wise ones.

The glory of God knocked Paul blind and he said it put the noon day sun in the shade. And when the saints of God burst forth and their bodies are changed they will eclipse the sun. Don't you think it will be great? Don't you think you had better take a degree of glory tonight?

He said to Peter, James and John, Don't tell any man about the vision until after I have gone to glory. So they saw something the rest did not know. Because they were nearer to God. They wanted God to let them down into the deep things of God. That teaches us a lesson, dear friends. There are degrees of glory. They that be wise shall shine as the firmament and they that be wise shall know when Jesus comes. Do you suppose God would not reveal these things to His waiting bride? I tell you yes. We know a few things now. We know it is very soon. "You are not left in the dark—you are all the children of light and of the day. You have been illuminated from heaven. You will not be overtaken by surprise. Are we ready, are we watching? Be ready to stand when the Son of Man comes. Watch and pray always. Watch the signs and watch the prophecies that you may be counted worthy to escape the awful tribulations and stand before the Son of Man when He comes. Watch and pray. You know the signs, you will not be over-taken as a thief because I am warning you. You are the children of day and you shall know. Glory to God!

So the Lord shows us now all these awful calamities coming on the earth. He says: Be ye not fearful when you see these awful things coming. Look up and rejoice. Lift your heads and see the break of day. The sun is rising. Lift up your heads. Rejoice, for your redemption draweth nigh. Glory!

The secret of the Lord is with those who love Him. Those He can trust. So God is revealing these things to us from day to day. We will not be surprised. When you see certain signs, know that it is even at your door. We know that now. We don't know the day or hour, but God gives us to understand we shall know a little while before we are taken up. And when you get where you cannot do anything else just stand, wait for the Son of Man to come and catch His waiting bride away.

Beautiful Fine Needle Work

Get this lesson, there are great degrees of glory. Don't you want to be the beautiful bride and stand before the King of Glory? Her clothes are so beautiful with fine needle work. And O how she loves her

Bridegroom. She doesn't worship anybody but Him. She is not trifling with many lovers, but He has become the fairest among ten thousand —[she is] willing to leave all and go with her strange lover.

Sometimes a lady here marries a stranger and there is lots of kicking. "If you go I will disinherit you." But she leaves her parents, home, money. O I love my lover best. He is mine and I am his. I will have to go and leave you. So she leaves everything and she gets into the ship and sails with her strange lover to a strange land, where she has never been, and among strange people that she has never known. And he is so proud of her. And she is so proud of him. He is strange to the world, but he is mine and I am his. I will be glad to go.

There are degrees of glory. He said, "The wise shall know." Don't think it strange that none of the wicked shall know about the coming of the Lord. Daniel saw the saints robed in white on land and sea, God scattering the Holy Ghost through them. Daniel, the wise, shall know. He reveals His secrets to the wise. Are you one of the wise? Is God letting you down into the deep things? Bless God He will! We are in the Holy Ghost school, going from one room to another, from one school to another, graduating, getting our diploma. God wants us to get down into the deep things. He reveals His secrets to us just like to those three. "Don't you tell any one until after I am raised from the dead." It was hid from the rest. That shows us, dear friends, there are degrees in glory. Some shall shine as stars and some will eclipse the sun. A great many people will not know when Jesus comes. The wise shall know when Jesus comes.

At that time there will be two sleeping in one bed, one will be taken and the other left; two grinding at the mill, one will be taken and the other left. Many people think they will know and they will be left. God is showing us these things and giving us this lesson. After Jesus went up they were all in the dark. They lost their faith. All power will be taken away when Christ has gone and the saints are gone. The devil will be let loose and the antichrist will begin to show his power. We find a type of this period in the story of the man that had the demons in him. The disciples could not cast them out. The father brought him to Jesus and said, The demons try to drown him; burn him and knock his brains out. Jesus cast the demons out and commanded that they enter no more into him. So the antichrist will burn some and drown some and knock the heads off of others as in the dark days. And then Jesus comes back, binds the devil and destroys the army of the antichrist—two-thirds of all the earth—and only one-third who went through all the fires trusting God the best they could are going to escape.

Chapter 16

The Resurrection
of the Bodies
# of Many Saints

THOU HAST ASCENDED ON HIGH, THOU HAST LED CAPTIVITY captive; thou hast received gifts for men; yea, for the rebellious also, that the Lord God might dwell among them (Psalm 68:18).

After all the life of Jesus, after all His mighty signs, and wonders, and miracles,"Behold the man," "Never man spake like this man," "What manner of man is this, that even the winds and the sea obey Him!" [1]

If He had stopped short at Calvary, or at going down into the cold grave, His work would have been a failure. Many people look only at the dead Saviour. They have only a dead religion: of form; and of works. They have no life, or power. Remember, Jesus brought life and immortality to light, to us, through the Resurrection. No, the grave could not hold him, though all hell was up in arms to hold Him cold in death. A hundred or more armed soldiers stood around His grave, for fear that his disciples would steal his lifeless body away. They also sealed the sepulchre with the governor's seal, and it was death to break that seal.

A mighty battle was fought. All the armies of heaven were engaged with the hosts of hell, in fierce array around the rock casket, or tomb, where the body of Jesus, our crucified Lord, lay cold in death. Hear the demons, "We have got Him, and we will hold Him captive. Where is your prince? Where is your King?" But hark, listen! The battle turns, victory is near, help is coming. The Lord God Almighty is coming Himself, with His great angel, that rolls back the stone from the sepulchre and sits upon it. His countenance was like lightning. His raiment white as snow, and for fear of Him the keepers did quake. They fell, and lay as dead men.

God, with His mighty presence, sent a great earthquake, and with a great shout over death, and hell, and the grave, we see the Conqueror come forth, holding the keys to unlock the prison house of the dead.

We see the women last at the cross, the first at the grave. The angel said, "Fear not ye: for I know that ye seek Jesus, which was crucified. He is not here: for he is risen, as he said. Come, see the place where the Lord lay. And go quickly, and tell his disciples that he is risen from the dead" (Matthew 28:5-7).

As they went with great joy, Jesus met them, saying, "Fear not, but go and tell my brethren that I will meet them in Galilee."

The women were commanded by the angels, and later by the Lord Himself, to preach the first news of the Resurrection.

No, dear reader, He is not dead. The Lord is risen indeed. Oh! praise God for a living Christ, a living church, and our Soon Coming King and Lord. Praise Him for the great marriage supper of the Lamb, that will soon take place in the air (1 Thessalonians 4:16-17).

Saints Come Forth
and Follow Their Master

The graves were opened and many of the bodies of the saints, that slept in their graves, arose and came out after His Resurrection, and went into the city, and appeared to many.

The Jewish church had forsaken the Lord, and He had taken His Spirit from her. For about four hundred years she was in darkness. There were no prophets, no priests, and no communication from heaven, until the birth of John the Baptist, and Christ's birth were announced.

It says "many of the saints," many would mean thousands or more, and we have every reason to believe that most of those saints were the prophets, and priests. Abraham, Isaac, Jacob, and Joseph; and those holy men of old, who spake as they were moved by the Holy Ghost, including John the Baptist, who had lately been murdered for Jesus' sake.

Oh! Praise God for the resurrection of these mighty men of old. Their bodies came up, and their spirits were united to them. They were living men, breathing, and walking, and their bodies were free from corruption. See them going through the streets of Jerusalem, going from one place to another, and making themselves known.

Oh! Praise God for the resurrection of our bodies, and that we shall know each other.

Yes, the devil held their bodies captive for hundreds of years in the grave. But see the mighty Conqueror break the chains, take them captive from the devil, and from the power of the grave, and leading captivity captive, take them away to some other world, where no doubt God is using them in some great way, for His glory.

He did not take them to heaven when He went, for no one had ascended to heaven. Those who are raised at His coming will be the first fruits of the Resurrection. But the spirits of the saints have gone to be with Christ since Pentecost. Paul says, I know, and am confident that when I am absent from the body I shall be present with the Lord.

He ascended on high and gave gifts to men. Yea, to the rebels also. Jesus did not have all power until after God raised Him from the dead. No one could have the gift of God, Eternal Life, until after he was born of the Spirit.

Jesus has all power. He was raised up with all power. The Holy Ghost was with the disciples, but Jesus said, "He shall be in you." When they were all together, Jesus met with them, and He opened their spiritual minds. He breathed on them, and said, "Receive ye the Holy Ghost." They received Him, and became partakers of the divine nature. They received the gift of God, were enlightened and cried out, "My Lord and my God." No one ever had that experience before that time. They were sons of God by the new birth. It was the gift of God, Eternal Life. "Yea, for the rebellious also." This is the most important of all gifts. For without this gift you can never get inside the Pearly Gates.

When the sinner stops his rebellion, and repents, God gives him faith to accept Christ. God gives him power to become a son of God, who are [is] born, not of man nor of the will of men, nor of flesh and blood, but by the power of God. He is then no longer a rebel, but a son, for he has received the gift of God, and has been born of the spiritual family record of God. His name has been written in the family record, by the finger of God, and it has been said, "This man was born in Zion." He has the finished work on Calvary for sin, and uncleanness. And he is now a child of God, ready for any or all of the gifts of the Pentecostal baptism, and power. He is God's man.

Jesus received gifts for men. When Jesus was giving His last blessing, on the mountain, before going up to heaven, He said to them, "Tarry at Jerusalem, until ye be endued with power from on high. Ye shall receive power after that the Holy Ghost has come upon you. Ye shall then be witnesses of me. All power is given unto me in heaven and in earth. Go ye into all the world and preach the gospel to every creature. These signs shall follow them that believe" (all that believe on me. These are some of the gifts that I will give to men.) "In my name shall they cast out devils, they shall speak with new tongues, they shall take up serpents, and if they drink any deadly poison it shall not hurt them, they shall lay hands on the sick and they shall recover." [2]

These were the last words our Saviour spake on earth, before He was taken up in a visible manner out of their sight. After that they got the promised baptism and greatest gift, they went forth preaching the word everywhere, the Lord working with them, confirming the word with the signs following.

They could not see the Lord in person like in days past, but saw the visible signs of His invisible presence.

These signs and gifts could be seen and heard with the natural eye and ear. Jesus was with them, with all gifts and signs, and miracles, and divers operations of the Spirit. With these He confirmed, and put His seal on the truth, and on their preaching.

Sat Like Cloven Tongues of Fire

At Pentecost He sent the promise of the Father. The Holy Ghost came as a rushing wind, and sat on all their heads, as cloven tongues of fire. These cloven tongues were a sign of the new tongues; they were tongues of fire and of the Spirit. For they were all filled with the Spirit, and began to speak as the Spirit gave them utterance.

It was the time of the great Jewish feast, and all the Jewish nations under heaven were gathered there, and they saw and heard the wonderful display of the Holy Ghost, and the gifts, and the glory of God.

They were amazed, saying, "What meaneth this, and how hear we every man in our own tongue wherein we were born?" Jesus had sent gifts down for men and women. The Holy Ghost had come to stay. He was given now without measure. God sent Peter down to Caesarea to hold a revival amongst the Gentiles; and while He was preaching the Holy Ghost fell on them that heard the Word, for they spake with tongues, and magnified God.

The Holy Ghost was poured out with all the gifts on the Gentile nations, just the same as at Pentecost on the Jews. "For the promise is unto you, and to your children, and to all that are afar off, even as many as the Lord our God shall call" (Acts 2:39). Oh! Praise God, beloved brethren, that takes in you and me.

Jesus sent these gifts, with all the Pentecostal power and glory. Our bodies are God's Power House, they are the channels for the Holy Ghost to flow out of like rivers of living water. "He spake of the Holy Ghost."

"That the Lord might dwell amongst them." This is the sign to the lost world, that God is with us, the signs of His invisible presence. We are a people to be wondered at. "Here Father am I, and the children thou hast given." We are for signs and wonders in Israel from the Lord of Hosts, that dwells in Zion—down here, not in heaven.

"He led captivity captive, and gave gifts unto men....He gave some, apostles; and some, prophets; and some, evangelists; and some, pastors and teachers" (Ephesians 4:8, 11). These imply, and include all the gifts, and workings of the Holy Ghost.

Why did He send this power and gifts to men, to His brethren, and to the church? He says for the perfecting of the saints, for the work of the ministry, for the edification of the body of Christ. To make the saints, God's men perfect; to lead them in the same Pentecostal power and gifts.

The ministers need it, and they must have the seal of the Holy Ghost, with all these signs, and gifts, to encourage them. They are the visible signs to the world, and seals to them, that God is with them, working together with them, confirming the word, with visible signs.

When the disciples were put into prison, and their lives were threatened, on account of the great power with them, in healing, and miracles, they were forbidden to preach in the name of Jesus; for they saw the power came through His name.

They came together, and they knew it was the power of God that caused [provoked] all their persecution. They knew if they had a form of religion, and denied the power, that they would have no more trouble. But, beloved, they said, "We will be true to God. We will preach the Word if we die." Then they prayed to the Lord, saying, "Lord, behold their threatenings: and grant unto thy servants, that with all boldness they may speak thy word, By stretching forth thy hand to heal; and that signs and wonders may be done by the name of thy holy child Jesus" (Acts 4:29-30).

You see these ministers needed power to give them boldness to stand up for Jesus, to preach all the words of this life.

His Presence and Power Miraculous

When they preached they knew they must see the signs in the meeting of the presence of the invisible Christ, who will be present to confirm the Word, and their message. Jesus had said, "I will be with you all the way even to the end of the world." Then like Peter they could say to those present, "This that you see and hear and feel, it is the promise of the Father, it is the Holy Ghost."

The Son was pleased with their prayer, and with their faith and courage, and the place was shaken—the building where they were assembled—and they were all filled with the Holy Ghost, and spake the Word with boldness.

Beloved, see, this was a greater baptism. They needed it to prepare them for the work they had to do. After this, they had greater success. God did mighty signs and wonders at the hands of the apostles; great fear fell on all the church, and on all that heard, and saw, these things. Multitudes of men and women came flocking to Christ, and were added to the Lord.

Multitudes means thousands. They came from Jerusalem, and all the cities round about, bringing their sick folk in beds, and cots; placing them along the streets, that the shadow of Peter passing by might overshadow them. You see that the power went forth from their bodies, like as when Paul laid handkerchiefs on his body, and sent them to the sick, and the devils or disease went out, and they were healed.

Oh! Praise God, I am a witness to these things. We see the same thing today, some of the greatest miracles of healing, and salvation I have ever seen have been done in the same way, hundreds of miles away. He gave gifts to men.

Read carefully the twelfth chapter of the first epistle to the Corinthians. Paul shows that the church is in possession of all the gifts, power, and calling and work of the Holy Ghost. That they are in the Body of Christ, His church.

Oh! Beloved, we ought to come up to this, in all places in these last days, when the bride is making herself ready. He says He does not want us to be ignorant concerning spiritual gifts, "Covet earnestly the best gifts," "Follow after charity," or love. "Desire spiritual gifts," for God has set them in the church.

Gifts for the rebellious also. Thank God, the sinner need no longer be rebellious, but fall at His feet, and settle the old account. He says He has a gift for you. Oh, "The Gift of God is Eternal Life" and then you are God's man. No longer a stranger or foreigner, but have been brought near by the blood of Christ. Through Him we will have access by one Spirit unto the Father. You are a citizen with the saints, and of the household of God; you are lively stones in the building that is being fitly framed together; an holy temple in the Lord.

Brother, you are a son, and an heir to all the Pentecostal blessings, gifts, and power. Press your claims at the Court of heaven.

Seek the Baptism of the Holy Ghost, and power. You can be a pillar in the temple of God, in, to go out no more. Be among the wise, that shall know of the Lord's coming. Among the wise that shall shine as the brightness of the firmament.

Let all that read this sermon take warning. "He that knoweth My will and doeth it not shall be beaten with many stripes" (Luke 12:47, author's paraphrase).

Chapter 17

The Marriage Supper
of the Lamb

BLESSED ARE THEY WHICH ARE CALLED UNTO THE marriage supper of
the Lamb (Revelation 19:9).

Oh, Beloved, have you been called? Let us be glad and rejoice,
and give honor to Him, for the marriage of the Lamb has come. The
bride must be arrayed in linen, pure and white.

Yes, his wife has made herself ready; see the King coming out
of His ivory palace, that he has ready to receive His bride. His garments are flooded with the sweet odors. They smell of myrrh, and
aloes, and cassia.

She is rejoicing in his love. Hearken! Oh, daughters! Beloved are
we the blessed that are called to the banquet? To this heavenly marriage supper in the skies? Oh, consider, and incline your ears to hear
the whispers of His love.

We must forget our own people, and our Father's house. Our
beloved Bridegroom is very jealous. We must love Him with our whole
heart, and our whole being. We must long for Him, so that He will
greatly desire our beauty. For He is our Lord, and we must worship Him.

We must be ready to leave all at any moment that the herald shall
shout, "Behold the Bridegroom. Behold, He cometh, go ye forth to meet
Him." Oh, are you ready to leave all to sail away with our beloved to
that heavenly kingdom, to those mansions in the City of Gold, that He
has been preparing and adorning for so many years, with all the
wealth, and jewels of heaven? Oh, that City of Gold!

Do our hearts leap for joy? Do we cry, "Come, oh come quickly,
my Redeemer, my Beloved and my King?" Oh! Most Mighty, with Thy
Glory, and Thy Majesty, Thou art fairer than all the sons of men! "Thy
throne, O God, is for ever and ever: the sceptre of thy kingdom is a
right sceptre" (Psalm 45:6).

Oh! Look at the lovely bride. They are all honorable women, king's daughters. Behold, on His right hand stands the queen robed in the shining glory of Ophir. The king's daughter is all glorious within: her clothing is of wrought gold. She shall be brought to the king in raiment of needlework.

The virgins, her companions that follow her, shall be brought unto her. Oh! Glory to God! Look at the virgins, the guests at the wedding, they shall go in with gladness, rejoicing with great joy, they will be brought into the King's palace.

Streets Like Transparent Glass

Oh! the very gates of solid pearl. The walls jasper, and the city is pure gold, like clear glass. The streets are pure gold, like transparent glass.

The very foundations are built and garnished with all manner of precious stones.

Oh! behold! Let us rise on the wings of faith, and in the Spirit take a view of our eternal home. The city lieth four square. Fifteen hundred miles long; fifteen hundred miles wide; fifteen hundred miles high. Oh, those pearly gates and jasper walls! How they shine in the glorious brightness and light of God, and the Lamb. Oh, beloved, if the outside is so glorious, what will it be to live in the city to roam through the Courts of Glory?

Our Lord says we shall go in with joy and rejoicing. Oh, our Lord will have many surprises for us, as He takes us through our mansions fair. We shall sit with Him in His throne, and be surrounded with all the brightness and glory of heaven.

We shall see the River of Life running out from beneath the Throne of God, like a sea of clear glass. There will be the nation of kings, with their gold crowned heads.

We shall eat of the Tree of Life, that bears twelve manner, or kinds of fruits every month. Oh, these beautiful trees on each side of the River. We shall eat of the fruit. Jesus said, "I say unto you, I will not drink henceforth of this fruit of the vine, until that day when I drink it new with you in my Father's kingdom" (Matthew 26:29). Yes, we shall eat and drink with our Bridegroom in His kingdom. Jesus said, "I appoint unto you a kingdom, as my Father hath appointed unto me; That ye may eat and drink at my table in my kingdom" (Luke 22:29-30). Oh, praise the

Lord, this is strong proof that the kingdom is literal, and natural. It shall be free from the curse of sin. "Blessed are they that are called to the marriage supper of the Lamb."

See the Feast, "The Lord will make a feast of fat things, a feast of wine on the lees, of fat things full of marrow, of wine on the lees well refined" (Isaiah 25:6, author's paraphrase). He will swallow up death in victory. And the Lord God Himself will wipe all tears from off all faces. The rebuke will be forever taken off His people.

Oh! Hasten the day when the kingdoms of this world shall become the kingdoms of our Lord, and His Christ, and He shall reign, and we shall reign with Him for the ages of ages. Oh, Blessed King! Come and take up Thy great power and reign.

We are now bearing the image of Adam, the first man, but our fleshly bodies will be changed, and made like unto His glorious body, our mortal body will be changed to an immortal body. Jesus ate with His disciples, after He arose from the dead, with the same body, and so will we, for we will be like Him.

Brethren, "We shall not all sleep, but we shall all be changed, In a moment, in the twinkling of an eye" (1 Corinthians 15:51-52). "Then we which are alive and remain shall be caught up together with them (the glorified and risen dead) in the clouds, to meet the Lord in the air: and so shall we ever be with the Lord" (1 Thessalonians 4:17).

The time is about up, when Jesus will come to take out a people for His bride, and will give her His name. Yes, we shall be called the bride, the Lamb's wife: she will be His pride and glory. He will be glorified in her through the ages of the ages.

As they travel through the many beautiful worlds, and He presents her, in all her beauty, she, in her pride and glory, points to her Royal Bridegroom, and tells of His wonderful redeeming love.

The Time Is at Hand

Yes, the time is at hand. Jesus has given us many signs, that we should know when to look for His return: when we should know that His coming is near, even at the doors. He said that the wise should know. "And they that be wise shall shine as the brightness of the firmament" (Daniel 12:3).

Oh, Beloved, are we watching? Are we waiting? Will we be ready to escape all the awful things that are coming on the earth? To many that are looking it will be a day of darkness, and there will be no light in it for them. He will come as suddenly as a flash of lightning, and we will be taken as quickly.

He will come with all the brightness of heaven. The saints will see all His glory, and will hear all the bells of heaven ringing, amidst the singing of the great angelic choir, they will be caught away, swallowed up in all this brightness and glory. But the poor lost world will sleep on, not knowing what has happened. Two will be sleeping in one bed, the one taken, and the other left. Two will be at the mill grinding, one taken, the other left. Two will be in the field, the one taken, the other left.

So suddenly shall this appear that they will not know it until too late: then they will realize what has happened, when they see that all these foolish cranks, these people, have disappeared.

No, the world is too blinded in darkness, and sin, she cannot behold the glory of the Rapture, as the saints go shouting through the air.

Hark! We might almost hear them marshalling the hosts of heaven. The angels tuning their harps of gold. We can almost see the banquet, the table spread for the marriage supper in the air. Many have seen the table, reaching across the skies. The great preparation is soon coming. Oh, dear reader, will you accept the invitation to the marriage supper in the skies? Oh! Glory to God, I will meet you there!

Chapter 18

Christ
and His Bride

AND TO THE ANGEL OF THE CHURCH IN PHILADELPHIA write; These things sayeth he that is holy, he that is true, he that hath the key of David, he that openeth, and no man shutteth; and shutteth, and no man openeth;

I know thy works: behold, I have set before thee an open door, and no man can shut it: for thou hast a little strength, and hast kept my word, and hast not denied my name.

Behold, I will make them of the synagogue of Satan, which say they are Jews, and are not, but do lie; behold, I will make them to come and worship before thy feet, and to know that I have loved thee.

Because thou hast kept the word of my patience, I also will keep thee from the hour of temptation, which shall come upon all the world, to try them that dwell upon the earth.

Behold I come quickly: hold that fast which thou hast, that no man take thy crown.

Him that overcometh will I make a pillar in the temple of my God, and he shall go no more out: and I will write upon him the name of my God, and the name of the city of my God, which is new Jerusalem, which cometh down out of heaven from my God: and I will write upon him my new name (Revelation 3:7-12).

The Philadelphian Church

Here Jesus Himself is giving John a description of the Philadelphian church, which name signifies love.

"A glorious church, not having spot, or wrinkle, or any such thing; but that it should be holy and without blemish" (Ephesians 5:27).

She must be a glorious church, not having spot or wrinkle or any such thing. Holy and without blemish. Oh! brother, it means much to be a member of this church.

The Book of Revelation is the most wonderful of the New Testament. Jesus had said to Peter in answer to his question, "And what shall this man do?" "If I will that he tarry till I come, what is that to thee? follow thou me" (John 21:21-22). The report went out that John would never die.

When John was quite old, the enemies of Christ tried to kill him. They threw him into a kettle of boiling oil, but the Lord did not let it hurt him. Then they were frightened, and banished him to the lonely isle called Patmos, and he was left there to die. He had been such a true witness for Jesus and His Word that it was the darkest hour of his life; but he was alone with God, filled with the Spirit.

The Book of Revelation is a wonderful book. About sixty-four years after John, and the other disciples, saw Jesus go up to heaven, He came back to earth, to John, and gave him great moving pictures of the church, from Pentecost. Oh, what power! What a force! What a light, in those dark days! All things are possible to him that believeth.

Jesus came back to John in all His kingly power and glory. He had been gone a long time. The change was so great that John felt so little in His presence that when he saw Him, he fell at His feet as one dead.

John said, He laid His right hand on me, saying, "Fear not, I am alive for evermore. John do you know me? We fished together, walked together, and slept together. Many times you have rested your weary head on my bosom." Can we imagine the joy when John heard the old voice of the Galilean, that had quieted their fears so often, when the sweet voice said, "It is I, do not be afraid. I have come back to bring you important messages, I want you to write all you hear, and send it to the churches."

The first three chapters of Revelation give the career of Christ's body, or church, from the time she was established at Pentecost down to the last Overcomer, and to the close, where the church is taken up to glory, and seated on the throne with Jesus, executing judgment on the lost world; and showing all that would take place down to the end of the one thousand years.

The first thing John heard was a great voice, like a trumpet. He looked to where the voice came from, and he saw seven golden candlesticks, representing the seven churches, or Christians down to the last. He saw Jesus in the midst of the candlesticks, in all His power, and glory.

His eyes were as a blaze of fire. His feet like a blazing furnace. His voice like the sound of many waters; in His right hand seven stars; out of His mouth went [a] two-edged sword. His countenance was like the sun shining in all its strength. Oh glory to God! What a Prince! What a King! What a living Wonder-working Power is our Christ, in His church, in us, beneath us, around us, like a wall of fire!

He shows us our greatest trials, and battles will be with the devil in the enemies of Christ, and His true church. But hear Him say, "Behold I will make them come, and fall at our feet, and acknowledge that God loves us, and that we are His true witnesses."

Christ is on trial for His honor and glory, as never before. When so-called "great preachers" are denying the atoning blood, and everything but the dead letter, hear Him say, "I hold the key. I will open for you." No man or power can close the door against us. We will keep His Word, and not deny His Name, or be ashamed of His works.

He warns us we will have trouble, be persecuted, misrepresented by false prophets, who call themselves Jews or great Christians, and leaders, but who are of the synagogue of Satan, who lie, and do not the truth.

Come out of the Laodicean church, and become a Philadelphian.

The Rapture of the Saints

The fourth chapter of Revelation shows the Rapture of the saints, and that their seat is on His throne. Jesus gives the description of the church all through. It applies and His message is to us who are now living on earth today.

The Laodicean church is the last, or great church of today, including all organizations, or bodies in the world, having a nice form of godliness, but denying the power thereof; "From such turn away."

There has been a falling away from the doctrine of Christ, and the Holy Ghost, and apostolic power, and wisdom, to a cold form, and to a teaching of the doctrines and traditions of men.

> And unto the angel of the church of the Laodiceans write; These things saith the Amen, the faithful and true witness, the beginning of the creation of God;
>
> I know thy works, that thou art neither cold nor hot: I would thou wert cold or hot.

So then because thou art lukewarm, and neither cold nor hot, I will spew thee out of my mouth.

Because thou sayest, I am rich, and increased with goods, and have need of nothing; and knowest not that thou art wretched, and miserable, and poor, and blind, and naked:

I counsel thee to buy of me gold tried in the fire, that thou mayest be rich; and white raiment, that thou mayest be clothed, and that the shame of thy nakedness do not appear; and anoint thine eyes with eyesalve, that thou mayest see.

As many as I love, I rebuke and chasten: be zealous therefore, and repent.

Behold I stand at the door, and knock: if any many hear my voice, and open the door, I will come into him, and will sup with him, and he with me.

To him that overcometh will I grant to sit with me in my throne, even as I also overcame, and am set down with my Father in his throne.

He that hath an ear, let him hear what the Spirit saith unto the churches (Revelation 3:14-22).

This is what concerns us. God is calling His people out of her. Thousands have heard the call, "Come out of her my people, that ye be not partakers of her sins, and that ye receive not of her plagues." The Last Call is going forth. The Lord is shouting in voice of thunder, through His bride, "Come out quickly." You may have time to be an Overcomer in the temple of my God, and of such He says, "He shall go out no more."

High Rank of the Family of God

The bride must graduate in the highest honors of the Holy Ghost. Those who sit on His throne will be the highest rank of all the whole family of God. They will be heirs of God, equal with Christ; they will have kingly power with Christ to rule the nations for one thousand years. They are called the wise, and are those that Daniel saw.

"And they that be wise shall shine as the brightness of the firmament; and they that turn many to righteousness as the stars for ever and ever" (Daniel 12:3).

The wise shall shine as the brightness of the firmament (there are degrees of glory, one of the sun, one of the moon), or as the stars for ever. We thought years ago that the winning of souls was the greatest work. "They that turn many to righteousness shall shine as the stars for ever and ever," but "The wise shall shine as the brightness of the firmament." They shall shine as the sun in my Father's kingdom.

None of the wicked shall know anything about when Jesus comes, but the wise shall know. Hear him shout, "To him that overcometh will I grant to sit with me in my throne, even as I also overcame, and am set down with my Father in his throne" (Revelation 3:21). Oh! Praise the Lord, the wise shall sit with Christ on his throne.

They shall know just when Jesus will come for his bride. They will be pillars in His temple, in his body, or church. They will be initiated into the deep things of God, and know his secrets. They will go in, to go out no more. Oh! Let us be sure that we are faithful and true, then He will save us in that hour of trial, or tribulation, that is coming on all the world.

He will come Himself to take His bride, to take us if we are part of His bride, to the marriage supper of the Lamb, in the skies.

He says, "I am coming quickly," or soon. Hold fast to all you have received till He comes. See that no man take your crown. Him that overcometh will I make a pillar in my church.

Watch and pray that you may be counted worthy to escape all these things that are coming on the earth, and to stand before the Lord.

A Royal Nation in Royal Robes

We are strangers in a strange land, but are princes in disguise, our royal robes shine, but the world can not see. They can not see the table our Father hath prepared for us, spread out in shining brightness, and snowy whiteness. It is covered with royal dainties, rich wine to make us glad, [and] meat to make us strong. Heavenly bread to keep us alive for evermore, and oil to make us shine, bright lights in this dark world.

Our enemies can not taste of the feast. Oh! Praise the Lord, He is calling out a people for a special purpose in these last days. He calls them the wise ones, a chosen generation, a called-out nation, from among the nations; a royal kingly nation, or nations of kings; an holy priesthood; a peculiar people, who confess that they are not of this world, for our citizenship and kingdom is not of this world. We confess we are pilgrims and strangers.

As lively stones we are built up a spiritual house. Oh! Glory to God. We are God's temple, in which He lives and moves, and He uses the clay to show His glorious presence, and that the world can see that the treasure is in our earthen vessels, and that it is all of God.

We are a holy priesthood to offer up spiritual sacrifices to God through Jesus Christ. We are a living church, a spiritual body of Jesus, the living Head. Christ is the head, and we are the living members of His body.

Christ is the Firstborn. It has pleased God through Jesus, the Captain of our salvation, to bring many sons and daughters into the kingdom; for He does not call us servants but sons; and because we are the sons of God, He hath sent forth the Spirit of His Son, into our hearts crying "Abba Father."

The Church of God, and of our Lord Jesus Christ, was set up on the Day of Pentecost, in a blaze of glory. It was built on the foundation laid by the apostles and prophets, Jesus Christ being the Cornerstone. The apostles were the pillars of 120 that were present and received the Pentecostal baptism, and of the three thousand that were saved, who received the gift of the Holy Ghost and became lively stones, and were placed in the building that day.

Oh! Blessed are those that are called to the marriage of the Lamb. Psalm 45 tells us, "Kings' daughters were among thy honourable women: upon thy right hand did stand the queen in gold of Ophir.... The king's daughter is all glorious within: her clothing is of wrought gold" (verses 9 and 13). "And his wife hath made herself ready" (Revelation 19:7).

The Rejoicing of the Angelic Hosts

Oh! Hear the shouts around the throne, from one end to the other, as the voice of a great multitude, as the voice of many waters, as the voice of mighty thunderings, shouting Alleluias, For The Lord God Omnipotent Reigneth! Oh! Beloved, what is all this about? Do we comprehend that we are causing all this rejoicing?

All heaven is waiting to hear the shout, "Go forth to meet her." There is something wonderful soon going to take place.

The Mighty God that inhabiteth Eternity, with all the heavenly hosts, have been waiting thousands of years for this great event. For the mystical body to come together. Christ our living Head, the bride the living body, for the marriage of the Son of God, the Great Jehovah. For the marriage of the Lamb has come.

Oh, dearly beloved, let us abstain from worldly lusts, which war against the soul. Let our words be few, and well chosen, let our conversation be in heaven, from whence we are expecting a message from the King, telling us that He is coming. We can almost hear the bugle call of the angels, getting the armies of heaven ready for marching, almost hear the angel choir, tuning their harps of gold, all heaven is getting excited.

"To him that overcometh will I grant to sit with me in my throne, even as I also overcame, and am set down with my Father in his throne."

Jesus has not yet taken His throne, will not do so until He takes up His bride.

This promise is only to the wise of the bridal party; those who will sit with Christ on His throne will have the highest rank of all the hosts of heaven. This is only promised to the Overcomers, in the last days, to those who will be taken up from among men. This is the close of the bride's career on earth.

In the first verse of the fourth chapter of Revelation, we see the church translated to heaven. John was carried to heaven, he represents the Rapture.

> Immediately I was in the spirit (or changed, as we will be in the twinkling of an eye); and, behold, a throne was set in heaven, and one sat on the throne. And he that sat was to look upon like a jasper...and there was a rainbow round about the throne (Revelation 4:2-3).

The brightest jewels are mentioned to help us to comprehend a little of the brightness, and splendor, of the glory of Christ, and His bride.

He saw Jesus taking His throne, and seating the bride with Him in the midst of the throne.

Out of the throne proceeded lightnings, and thunderings, and voices: and there were seven lamps of fire burning before the throne, which are the seven Spirits of God. And before the throne there was a sea of glass like unto crystal; and in the midst of the throne, and round about the throne, were four beasts full of eyes before and behind.

The Glory of the Bride

The description of these beasts is symbolic of power, the wings and the eyes, signifying they were full of light, power and knowledge. They are so swallowed up in sunlight of glory that their crowns can not be seen.

Now these are not beasts, but the Overcomers, shining as the brightness of the sun; seated with Christ on His throne, just like he promised.

We see the twenty-four crowned heads seated around the throne, as if in council, but not on the throne. We hear these Overcomers shouting the loudest praises to the Lamb, and to the Lord God Almighty, Who was, and is, and Who has come to take His great power, and to reign.

When the Overcomers give glory to Him that sitteth on the throne, who liveth for ever and ever (Revelation 19:4). The Overcomers do not take part, but the four and twenty elders fall before the throne, and worship Him that sits on the throne, casting their crowns at His feet, saying, "Thou art worthy, O Lord, to receive honor, glory, and power." You see the beasts, or Overcomers on the throne did not fall down, but the others fell down in honor of what the living creatures had said.

In Revelation 5:8-10, we read:

> And when he had taken the book, the four beasts and four and twenty elders fell down before the Lamb, having every one of them harps, and golden vials full of odours, which are the prayers of saints.

> And they sung a new song, saying, Thou art worthy to take the book, and to open the seals thereof: for thou wast slain, and hast redeemed us to God by thy blood out of every kindred, and tongue, and people, and nation;

> And has made us unto our God kings and priests: and we shall reign on the earth.

You see the living creatures or rather Overcomers, and elders fall down before the Lamb, having every one of them harps of gold, and golden vials full of odors, which are the prayers of the saints. Oh! Hear the shouts of the Overcomers with the elders, "Thou art worthy, for thou wast slain, and hast redeemed us to our God, by thy blood, out of every kindred, and tongue, and people, and nation, and hast made us unto our God kings and priests, and we shall reign on the earth."

In the thirteenth verse, we hear all the hosts of heaven raise a shout giving glory to Him that sitteth on the throne, and the four living creatures say, Amen. And the four and twenty elders fell down and worshipped him that liveth for ever and ever.

When the Overcomers said amen, the elders fell down and worshipped, but the living creatures did not fall down, showing that they were redeemed by his blood from all nations, and were clothed with the highest honor, and power equal with Christ, in power and glory.

In the sixth chapter of Revelation you see the living creatures, the Overcomers, on the throne with Christ executing judgments on the earth, during the Great Tribulation. As one after another shouts, "Come and see," one judgment after another comes on the earth. "Do ye not know that the saints shall judge the world?" (1 Corinthians 6:2). And that saints shall judge fallen angels.

They shall come back with Christ to fight the last great battle, when the antichrist, and all his army shall be destroyed; after which we shall reign kings and priests for one thousand years. When all the residue of men shall seek after the Lord, and all the Gentiles shall call on His Name. Oh, hasten the day when the knowledge of God shall cover the earth, as the waters cover the great and mighty deep.

Chapter 19

Dancing in the Spirit is Victory for the Lord's Hosts

DAVID DANCED WITH ALL HIS MIGHT BEFORE THE LORD. THE Word is full of dancing. Where dancing in the Bible is mentioned, it always signifies victory for the Lord's hosts. It was always done to glorify God. The Lord placed the spirit of power and love of the dance in the church, and wherever the Scripture speaks of dancing it implies that they danced by inspiration, and were moved by the Spirit, and the Lord was always pleased, and smiled His approval; but the devil stole it away and made capital of it. In these last days when God is pouring out His Spirit in great cloudbursts and tidal waves from the flood gates of heaven, and the great River of Life is flooding our spirit and body and baptizing us with fire and resurrection life, and divine energy, the Lord is doing His acts, His strange acts, and dancing in the Spirit and speaking in other tongues, and many other operations and gifts. The Holy Ghost is confirming the last message of the coming King, with great signs and wonders, and miracles. If you read carefully what the Scripture says about dancing, you will be surprised, and will see that singing, music and dancing has a humble and holy place in the Lord's church. "Let them praise his name in the dance: let them sing praises unto him with the timbrel and harp" (Psalm 149:3). "Praise him with the timbrel and dance: praise him with stringed instruments and organs" (Psalm 150:4). "Then shall the virgin rejoice in the dance, both young men and old together" (Jeremiah 31:13).

(2 Samuel 6:14-23). David danced before the Lord with all his might; his wife did not like it, she scolded him and made light of him, said he was dancing before the maidens like a lewd fellow, made out as if he was base and low, but he answered, I was not dancing before men, but before the Lord; showing that he had lost sight of the world and what they thought or said, but was moved and controlled entirely by the Holy Ghost for the Glory of God. All the great company was blessed but Michal, and she was stricken with barrenness till the day of

her death, so you see she sinned in making light of the power of God in the holy dance (just as some do today), and attributed it to the flesh or the devil. They always lose out, and many are in darkness till death.

The news of King David's great victory, how he had killed the giant Goliath and destroyed the great army of the Philistines, spread quickly over the land, and as David returned from the slaughter the women came out of all the cities of Israel, singing and dancing, to meet the king, some with joy and instruments of music. Now notice, in all their cities the women went out in the streets and danced with their music; men are not mentioned there, just maidens, and women danced unto the Lord in honor of God, and the king prompted by the Spirit of God to praise Him in the dance. It took courage to honor the king in this way, but the Lord smiled His approval by having it written by holy men of old, and sent down to us in His precious Word.

"And he stood up, and leaped and praised God" (Acts 3:8; author's paraphrase). Paul said, "Stand upright on thy feet. And he leaped and walked" (Acts 14:10).

"And Miriam the prophetess...took a timbrel in her hand; and all the women went out after her with timbrels and with dances. And Miriam answered them, Sing ye to the Lord, for he hath triumphed gloriously; the horse and his rider hath he thrown into the sea" (Exodus 15:20-21). God has never done a greater miracle nor demonstrated His presence in so great a cloud of glory as at this time. While under the inspiration and light of His presence their whole bodies and spirits going out in love, the whole multitude of women, Miriam the prophetess and leader, leading them forth to praise the Lord with dancing, shouting and music, singing a new song just given by the Spirit that had never been sung, do you call that foolishness? No, they were praising the Lord in the dance and song as they were moving in and by the mighty power of God.

Moses also led the hosts in the same way, with music and dancing, and a new song given for the occasion by the Spirit. So the Holy Ghost is falling on the saints of God today, and they are used the same way. Those who never danced one step are experts in the holy dance, and those who do not know one note from another, are expert musicians in playing many different instruments of music, and often the sound of the invisible instruments are heard from the platform, the sounds can be plainly heard all over the house. And I say in the fear and presence of God, the singing and demonstration puts the fear of God on the people, and causes a holy hush to come over the people. The strange acts are coming more and more, showing they are something new, and that Jesus is coming soon, and the Lord is getting His bride ready to be translated, and dance and play at the great marriage of the Lamb, which will soon take place, for the bride is making herself ready.

(Luke 15:25-3; author's paraphrase). His elder son was in the field. When he came near the house he heard music and dancing; he asked what does all this mean? They said, "Thy brother has come home, and thy father has killed the fatted calf, because he has received him safe and sound, and he was angry and would not go in, but the feast and rejoicing went on just the same." The Father said, "It is meet that we should be merry and rejoice, for thy brother who was dead and who was lost, and we have received him safe and sound." All will agree with me, this was an old fashioned Holy Ghost revival. The lost son is a sinner whom the Spirit brought out of darkness to light, the saints are filled with the Spirit.

I was very slow to accept the dancing in the Spirit, for fear it was in the flesh, but I soon saw it was the "cloud of Glory" over the people that brought forth the dancing, and playing invisible instruments. The sounds of sweet, heavenly music could often be heard. Several times I asked that those of the congregation, who heard this music from the platform (where they knew there were no instruments to be seen) be honest and raise their hands. Many hands went up from saints and sinners. The stillness of death went over the people when they heard the sounds of music, accompanied with the heavenly choir. Often a message in tongues was given in one or more languages and the interpretation. As I saw the effect on the people by the Holy Ghost, in convincing them that they were in the presence of God, I concluded that this is surely the Lord's strange work, and His strange acts. I saw as many as nine of the most noted ministers dancing at one time on the platform; they danced single, with their eyes closed; often some fell, slain by the mighty power of God. These things convinced me. I also saw men and women who have been crippled join in the dance, with wonderful grace. One lady who was on crutches five years, who got healed in her seat, afterwards danced over the platform, singing heavenly music. The virgins, the young men, and the old men, all join in the dance together. Praise the Lord. "Let us be glad and rejoice, and give honour to him, for the marriage of the Lamb is come, and his wife hath made herself ready" (Revelation 19:7). The Lord is quickening our mortal bodies for the translation.

Chapter 20

Prepare for War

FOR, BEHOLD, IN THOSE DAYS, AND IN THAT TIME, WHEN I shall bring again the captivity of Judah and Jerusalem,

I will also gather all nations, and will bring them down into the Valley of Jehoshaphat....

Proclaim ye this among the Gentiles; Prepare war, wake up the mighty men, let all the men of war draw near; let them come up:

Beat your plowshares into swords, and your pruning hooks into spears: let the weak say, I am strong (Joel 3:1-2, 9-10).

But in the last days it shall come to pass, that the mountain of the house of the Lord shall be established in the top of the mountains, and it shall be exalted above the hills; and people shall flow into it.

And many nations shall come, and say, Come, and let us go up to the mountain of the Lord, and to the house of the God of Jacob; and he will teach us of his ways, and we will walk in his paths: for the law shall go forth of Zion, and the word of the Lord from Jerusalem.

And he shall judge among many people, and rebuke strong nations afar off; and they shall beat their swords into plowshares, and their spears into pruninghooks: nation shall not lift up a sword against nation, neither shall they learn war any more.

But they shall sit every man under his vine and under his fig tree; and none shall make them afraid: for the mouth of the Lord of hosts hath spoken it (Micah 4:1-4).

These two quotations from Joel and Micah sound a little contradictory. I have heard people say so. But the statements refer to two different parties and times.

The first, "Beat your plowshares into swords and your pruning hooks into spears" means "Get ready for battle," and it refers to this present time, a time of war.

The second, "Beat your swords into plowshares and your spears into pruning hooks" [means] "Get ready for a time of great farming."

The one to prepare for the greatest battle the world has ever heard of; the others to the time when war shall be no more.

The first text in this sermon, "Prepare for war; Wake up the mighty men of war. Let the nations gather together for battle," refers to this time of the end that we are now living in, when the Gentile time is full or closing.

Bound in the Great River Euphrates

We have every reason to believe that the four angels are loosed that were bound in the great River Euphrates, that were prepared to slay the third part of men. They are doing their work of destruction now in Turkey. All Europe is stirred and ready to go forth at any moment in deadly battle with each other.

You see the awful slaughter, massacre, deadly hatred, causing them to kill and destroy each other. God has risen up like a mighty man of war. He shall roar and shout out from Jerusalem till all nations are gathered in deadly combat, till the blood flows like a river.

Even now cholera, smallpox and other deadly pestilence and famine is raging, joining in the deadly work of destruction, which will go on till the dead will cover the land. The dead will lie unburied, food for all the wild beasts and vultures. The Lord hath spoken, for their sins have reached unto heaven, and God is turning His wrath and vengeance loose on a guilty, God-defying world.

In the text in Joel the call is primarily to the Holy Land, where the great battle of God Almighty will be fought. The battle of the great Day of God while the angel is standing in the sun, calling all the fowls of the air to come to the supper of the Great God, to eat the flesh of all the mighty men, the great men of the world, and the rich men. They are invited to eat and drink the blood and get fat on the flesh, on the carcasses of kings and princes of the world, who will soon fall in the notable Day of the Lord.

The Lord shall awake and shout out as a man of war. He shall roar out of Zion, and shall utter His voice from Jerusalem. The heavens shall shake and the earth, when the nations are gathering for this great battle with the Lamb and His army from heaven.

John says, "I saw heaven opened, and beheld a white horse, and Him that sat upon him. His eyes were as a flame of fire. On His head were many crowns, and He was clothed in a vesture dipped in blood. And the armies which were in heaven followed Him on white horses, clothed in white linen, white and clean" (Revelation 19:11-14; author's paraphrase).

Oh, praise the Lord! the saints have been translated to heaven. The marriage of the Lamb and His bride has taken place, with shouting and hallelujahs that have shaken all heaven and earth. The great marriage supper, with all its grandeur, and glory, and greatness is over. And they have been with the Lord executing judgments on the earth during the awful Tribulation.

Now the cup of wickedness is full. They have defied the God of heaven long enough. He has stood up in His wrath. All nations of the earth are gathering to the Valley of Jehoshaphat. The Lord of Lords and King of Kings, with all His armies of heaven comes riding in triumph, down through the skies. Enoch saw the Lord coming with ten thousand of His saints. The antichrist has gathered his army and is about to destroy God's children. They will gather all their armies together against Jerusalem to fight, but then the Lord comes from heaven and fights this great battle. The saints do not have to fight, the Lord Himself does the fighting.

After this great battle there will never be another sword or weapon of war used.

The Millennial Kingdom Set Up

Then the Millennial Kingdom is set up, and Satan will be chained during that thousand years. During that time the curse, and its effects, including all weeds, thistles, and that which would produce disease, etc., have been taken away. "Nothing shall hurt or destroy in all My Holy Mountain" (Isaiah 11:9; author's paraphrase). The time is coming when they shall cease to make war, and the devil is taken out of the hearts of the people.

Today they are just like wild beasts thirsting for each other's blood. They are burying the living and the dead together. Pestilence also has already begun its deadly havoc.

Did you ever hear of a great war breaking out so quickly? For years past the most talented men have been inventing to see who could get the most deadly weapons.

God has been holding back the tidal waves and the other destructive forces. His angel has shouted back, "Wait till the servants of God are sealed with the seal of God."

The division of the Book of Joel into chapters is bad. The first verses of the third chapter are a continuation of the last verses of the second chapter and should not be divided from them.

In the last days "I will pour out my Spirit" (Joel 2:28). Baptize with the Holy Ghost, and scatter the power of the Holy People.

God says, "I will rise up in My wrath in that day." When the judgments of God are in the earth some will repent. In the last days I will pour out of My Spirit. God says wake up the heathen.

God is sealing His saints, but that sealing time is pretty nearly over.

That they speak in new tongues is a sign that the Lord is coming.

"The power of the Holy People shall be scattered" (see Daniel 12:7; author's paraphrase). These are they that are clay in the Potter's hand. They are just clay, having no control of themselves at all. God Almighty speaks through them, "With stammering lips and other tongues will I speak unto this people, but for all that they will not hear" (Isaiah 28:11; 1 Corinthians 14:21; author's paraphrase).

Proclaim and tell it to the people. Blow the trumpet. Sound the alarm in the Holy Mountain. What is the danger? The Day of the Lord is coming, it is near at hand.

God's people are blowing the trumpet. They are sounding the alarm in Zion. What is the signal of danger? The great Day of the Lord is near.

It is time for the saints to get this knowledge if they do not already know it. How can we give the signal if we do not know? How could we warn the people of danger?

If they escape when the sword is coming, good. But warn them anyhow. If we do not warn them their blood will be on our hands. Wake up the heathen. Call up your mighty men. Call the soldiers into line. Get them ready. Get the weapons of war ready for the world's great conflict. There never has been anything like it, nor ever will be again.

A Great Dearth in Steel

There will be a scarcity of steel. They can not make enough of it. The nations are all the time building new war ships, and manufacturing so many deadly weapons. It takes a good deal of steel to make these warships. Such monster vessels. Each nation trying to build the largest ships, and invent the most deadly weapons.

Still, they are crying, "Peace, peace." Right in the midst of this false peace and security, death and war and destruction have come like a whirlwind.

There is a lack of steel. Where are they going to get it? Pretty soon they will not be able to meet the demand for it. Then men will be hunting around in the farm yards, old barns, stables, and sheds, everywhere for old plowshares and pruning hooks, for everything that they can beat into swords and spears to kill their neighbors with.

The time is coming in this glorious America when parties and factions will rise up—Labor against Capital, and other parties and factions. There will be no safety to him that goes out or goes in. And at that time they will not be able to buy or sell, unless they have the mark of the beast [Revelation 13]. It will be death, and to have the mark of the beast will mean the second death [Revelation 20].

There will be no safety or hiding place to him that goes out or in.

"As if a man did flee from a lion, and a bear met him; or went into the house, and leaned his hand on the wall, and a serpent bit him" (Amos 5:19).

It is implied [in Amos 5:19] that the land will be infested with poisonous serpents, reptiles, and insects, and they will be turned loose among the people, with their deadly power to bite, sting and destroy.

So that if you run away from the sword and pestilence, and try to hide in the house, you will lay your hand on the wall, and be bitten by a deadly serpent. There will be no safety to him that goes in or out.

There will be awful deadly hatred among the people, and they will be banded together hand in hand, and they will make weapons of steel with which to kill and destroy one another.

I read not long ago that the powers were crying out because of the scarcity of steel. Your neighbor will be hunting round for a piece of old steel to kill his neighbor with.

In Europe now they are calling out young men and boys to fight and to be destroyed.

It is time to wake up from the sleep of death and call on God to give you life.

According to the Word of God, and the signs of the times, we are now living in the commencement of these awful times, when many who read these lines will see a great deal more than I have written. You and your children will go down in death or go through this dreadful time of trouble such as never has been nor ever will be again.

Many of the best Bible students say that the eleventh chapter of Daniel refers to the Sultan, or ruling powers of Turkey.

"He shall plant the tabernacles of his palace between the seas in the glorious holy mountain; yet he shall come to his end, and none shall help him" (Daniel 11:45).

And they think that the book of Obadiah also refers to him.

The passage in Daniel does not refer to the antichrist, for he will not be revealed, or take his power till after the hinderer is taken away, till Christ takes out a people for His name from among the Gentiles, till He comes and takes His bride.

The End in the Time of the End

He shall come to his end in the time of the end, and at that time Michael, the great prince, shall stand up for his people, and all will be delivered whose names are written in the Book of Life, and the wise, who know these things shall shine as the brightness of the firmament.

The way the war is raging against Turkey it looks like she might lose her capital, Constantinople, and be compelled to leave her headquarters almost any day. How natural it would be for her to transfer her government to the Holy Land, of which she still has control, in haste; she could occupy almost any building for that purpose.

It is reported that the Turks are building a large palace or building and they are keeping it quiet, and will not tell anyone what it is for.

"He shall plant the tabernacles of his palace between the seas, in the glorious holy mountain; yet he shall come to his end, and none shall help him."

But he will not stay there very long; little by little, he will go down till he is entirely destroyed.

The Holy Land was to be trodden down of the Gentiles until the time of the end. Then and at that time Christ will come. The Jews will flock to Jerusalem and again possess the Holy Land.

Most of those that have gone through the Tribulation will have had enough and they will be ready to listen to the voice of that prophet.

If the angels are loosed it will not be long before we take our flight. When these things begin to come fast, we shall soon be taken out of the world. The worst trouble will come after the saints are taken out. The antichrist will deny the blessed Christ, and cause people to take his mark or to be put to death. Those who do not go up with Christ will have to go through this or go down in it.

Jesus comes to take a people out for His name, for His bride. He comes and takes her away to the heavens. The great marriage supper takes place, after which they will be sitting with Christ on His throne and helping to execute judgment during this awful Tribulation.

Look at the awful death and carnage, and destruction if you do not go up with the bridal company.

Those who go up when Christ comes are the Lamb's wife. He returns to build up the waste places of Jerusalem. The soil will all be fertile then, and the people will not need to do much work. It will be like a holy camp meeting all the time during the Millennial Age.

The first time Jesus comes none see Him but the bride. The world hates her, and cares nothing for her, and Jesus is going to take her away.

Christ will come as quickly as the lightning flashes from the East to the West, just that quick He will snatch His bridal company away, while the world sleeps in a drunken stupor.

But the next time He comes all will know it. "Every knee shall bow and every tongue shall confess," every eye shall see Him, and every slanderous tongue will have to confess before the world that these were God's chosen vessels.

This honor belongs to the saints. They will have to confess that we were right and that they were wrong. God is very proud of His bride. Children of God now deny themselves many of the things of the world, but we are heirs of the kingdom, though many of us are poor in this world and having hard times. There is going to be a change in this old world. God is calling you to behold. Don't go a step further. Don't step over the mangled body of Christ any more or it may be the last time.

A White Horse Bridal Procession

The first time the bride will be caught away, the second time she will come riding on white horses. Jesus will stand on Mount Olivet and they that pierced Him shall see Him. You know now down in your hearts that Jesus is the Christ. That we people are every one in earnest. That we hear something more than natural men hear. The wisdom we get from God who gives liberally. That has been my prayer more than anything else, "Give me wisdom." Almost a blind man can see if he looks at the signs of the times.

Daniel says the wise shall know when the Lord comes.

You may say I don't believe. You don't want to believe and that day will overtake you as a thief in the night. None of the wicked shall understand the signs of Jesus' coming. Ye who are children of the light shall know and that day will not overtake you unexpectedly. God gave Daniel a picture of the lost world, none of whom should know when He comes.

Who are the wise? Those who know the time of the Lord's coming. "And they that be wise shall shine as the brightness of the firmament; and they that turn many to righteousness as the stars for ever and ever" (Daniel 12:3). They that be wise shall know.

This is a wonderful message; now you can have your choice.

The greatest vengeance and pent up wrath of God will be poured forth on those that take the mark of the antichrist.

If we trust in God we can have faith so that none of these things shall hurt us.

Look, dear children of the Living God. Look, our redemption is near, even at the door. Oh, God, the sleeping virgins to awake, and flee to Christ, to get the Baptism of the Holy Ghost, to get sealed with the Spirit of promise, to get ready to take the flight in the air.

Oh, accept the invitation to the marriage supper of the Lamb. He will come like a flash of lightning from the East. We will go in a moment, we will arise to meet Him in the sky.

Don't be looking to the grave. Look, for behold He cometh. Oh, Glory to God in the highest. Come, Oh Redeemer, come quickly.

Chapter 21

Fear God and
Give Glory to Him,
for the Hour of His
Judgment Has Come

REVELATION 14:6-7. WE HAVE HERE SOME THINGS JOHN SAW. HE was carried away in a trance, and he was not hypnotized either. He saw an angel; he did not simply think so, but he saw it, flying in the midst of heaven, having the everlasting Gospel to preach; and saying, "Fear God and give glory to Him."

An angel flying through the earth, preaching the everlasting Gospel applies to us today in a wonderful way. We are living in the last days right in the end of this glorious dispensation. God is calling out a people from among men, preparing the bride whom Jesus is coming to receive as His own. God is calling His servants for the ministry of the Gospel of His kingdom. They go over the land with swiftness. They are called eagles. The eagle has great power and soars over every difficulty. It is so with God's children in these days. He gives us strength and courage such as has never been before.

We are sent as angels to sound the trumpet. When God calls, we have to go; skip across the ocean, running, flying, soaring over the world. Nothing can pull us down. God is calling us to give this old world the Last Call. He is taking men and women He can trust with His power to show up His goods to the world. A drummer [salesperson] shows the goods and secures orders. If he did not show up the goods he would not get the orders. People want to see the goods before they purchase.

So God calls us to show the samples; not only to tell what God can do, put Him to the test and show what He can do. We must be clothed with the power of the King, showing such signs and wonders as the world has never seen. That will put the fear of the Lord on all those who see and hear, we have a great responsibility, as never before. The message is, "Fear God and give glory to Him; for the hour of His judgment is come." Worship God, who made the heavens and the earth, the sea and all that therein is. Worship Him as never before. There are as many gods being worshipped in America today as among the heathen. The God of heaven is left in the shade and the Lord Jesus Christ thrown down by many professing Christians. Give glory to Him, Him, Him, the God of heaven, worship Him, and give glory to Him, for the hour of His judgment is come. That time is here. Fear God and give glory to Him. What is the message we are to give? Jesus is coming soon. God has given out the invitation to the marriage supper of His Son. We are invited to the feast, and having our wedding garments made. There is everything to coax the bride away from her Father's house, from everything that binds her.

What of the Morning? What of the Night?

Gather yourselves together. Those who follow him, gather yourselves together, despised and rejected. All men speak evil of this sect. Seek righteousness, meekness and power from God. Hide you away. Watchman, what of the morning? Glory to God! The sun is rising in the East. He is coming! What of the night? The night is coming soon. Death and destruction are coming; the judgments of God are coming. Blow ye the trumpet in Zion. Sound the alarm in the Holy Mountain. Let all the people tremble. Why are the people going to get alarmed and tremble? What is the danger? The armies of the devil are gathering. Hide, hide away in the rock from the wrath of God which is coming upon the earth. My God! warn the people. Let them tremble on account of their sins. We have to blow the trumpet, the signal of danger. We have to give the warning and let the people know. The angel choir is getting ready. His people are being trained down here to sing the song of the redeemed. May the people tremble; may the fear of God come upon them; there is a great day coming; a day of black darkness; black as midnight. God's judgment is going to burst upon this earth. Give the signal of danger. The great Day of the Lord is coming; it is near at hand; He is at the door. If we know it, help us to tell it!

The ancient cities had great walls around them, and watchmen placed day and night upon the walls. If they saw an army approaching, an enemy coming, or any danger threatening, they blew the trumpet, giving the warning to the men of war in the city who understood the signal, and the people could escape. If the watchman did not give the signal the blood of the people was on their heads. Watchman, if you do not warn and the enemy comes in and takes them, their blood will be upon your heads. God puts us upon the walls of Zion. Jesus is coming in this generation. The young people will not be old when He comes; according to His Word, the time is near. We are all for Him or against Him. How can you give the signal of danger if you do not know it? Worship God and give glory to Him, the God of heaven. If you blow the trumpet right, it will arouse the people. Then if they sleep on, your hands will be free from blood.

There never was such a responsibility on the people of God as there is today. There never was such a time for Jesus Christ to be held up as He is today. Gods of science and nature and other kinds are on the earth today. At a gathering of twenty-three ministers in Boston, only three accepted the Divinity of Christ. We have to drop all side issues and hobbies and everything but Jesus; we must hold up Jesus.

In these days, He is being crucified a thousand times worse than on the cross. In these days, His honor and His glory are at stake. Stand by Him and defend His Holy Name. Hold up the fountain of Calvary opened wide; it cleanses from the effect of sin; it has power today, flowing from the wounded side of Jesus. Let us stand by Him in the battle against the world, the flesh, and the devil. Men may call us every name that can be invented, hypnotists, fanatics, and cranks, trying to strike those who are stepping out on God's promises. How the heart of Jesus must bleed! If we stand firm with Him, He will let the people know the work is of God. Stand firm; set your face like a flint. Prove the Word; He says He will stand by us to deliver us in the hour of temptation, and in the hour of tribulation, coming on the earth. Be true to Him; hold up the atonement and the power of the blood. He will save us from the black darkness that is settling over the world.

We have to stand by Him and hold up Jesus, though men and devils howl and speak against Him and the wonderful works of the blessed Holy Spirit. Can He find men and women, messengers, who will interpret the Word aright and show what the mighty power of God is? He says if we will stand by Him now and blow the trumpet, the Word of God will girdle the earth. God will be here to judge His people and the glory of heaven be brought down to fight our battles. Let us hold up Jesus. Don't talk about side issues, getting a bone of contention and talking about it. When people know Him, they will know what to do, what to wear, how to get married, and live when they are married. Preach Jesus. Glory to God! People will not change their ideas to please you; God Almighty has to show them. These things break up meetings and the people lose their power. Lift up Jesus. It is not by might or by power; it is the Almighty God doing the work, we must show up what He is doing. Let us stand by Him this little time when the command goes forth to blow the trumpet. The great Day of the Lord is near at hand, at the door; give the signal of danger and He will back it up by signs and wonders. We must have the signs and wonders, if we are preaching the Word, to get people to believe on Him. They are worshipping a mystical God. Doctrine of devils; the wrath of God must come upon those who follow these; the blood will come up to the horses' bridles. God is holding back the four winds to give us a chance to blow this trumpet and He will back it up with power. The time is near at hand. There are idol temples set up in this land; and a man sets himself that he is God. They are getting ready; everywhere, federations are forming.

Don't go into the federations; keep out of it. Don't be afraid of their threats. Fear God, for the hour of His judgment is at hand. Cannot you see these things? People are preaching the Fatherland [Fatherhood] of God and brotherhood of man, and leaving the blood out entirely. Don't be afraid of their threatenings; fear God; He will deliver. We see these things, see them everywhere; Christ is at hand. Worship the God of heaven. Who stands for Jesus, the lowly Nazarene? Who will stand for Him, when every one is pointing the finger of derision? There are millions of professing Christians today, who are denying the Lord Who bought them. They deny the divinity of Christ; and deny the power of the Holy Ghost. You can have the knowledge of these things, if the blood cleanses you. You may feed the poor and all that; if you have not the Spirit of God, all you do outside of Jesus Christ will never build a ladder to take you to heaven. You cannot go except through Christ. If you are in the flesh, and the Spirit of God dwelleth not in you, then you are a reprobate. Little children, you do know God, praise His Name; give God the glory.

God has revealed by the Spirit that the Laodicean church will be spewed out. They have a name to live and are dead, spiritually; they have a beautiful outside form, but deny the power of the Holy Spirit: from such turn away. They do not know the Holy Ghost, nor the blood that bought them. They stand off and say people are hypnotized, mesmerized, or drunk, as they said on the Day of Pentecost. They do not want to investigate; they are afraid of being called fools by the world. I would rather be a fool in God's hands than be for the devil. Wouldn't you? David danced before the ark with all his might, yet they call us cranks because we dance. God give us more cranks. Don't you see the darkness in the land? None of these people, judging by their actions, know anything about the Holy Ghost. When they come near us there is a fear on them; they don't want to believe it. God help us to know the difference between animal excitement and the power of God. It is the power of God; yet they call it hypnotism when they see people laid out under His mighty power.

Don't you see how little they know of Jesus? He set us the example. He cast out demons, healed the sick, sent the Holy Ghost down upon His disciples, and they staggered like drunken men and they spoke in tongues. They were "Drunken, but not with wine; they stagger, but not with strong drink" (Isaiah 29:9). This is the way today. John the Baptist prophesied that Jesus would baptize with the Holy Ghost and fire. What do you know about that? When people see the Holy Ghost working, they say we are crazy.

God's people are alive. Give glory and worship to God, for the hour of the judgment is at hand. You see some people worship a dead Christ, giving heed to doctrines of men and devils. There is a power in education, wealth, and fine sermons. God help us to preach in the power of the Holy Ghost. They set Christ aside. If they had the blood of Christ applied to their hearts, how they would love God! Then they would know the power of the blood, and the power of the Holy Spirit. Christ said, "I will send the promise of the Father; and, ye shall receive power after that the Holy Ghost is come upon you."[1] Then ye shall work miracles. Preach my Word and I will be with you. He is with us. If you will believe right you shall cast out demons—legions are all around us—you shall lay hands on the sick, and they will not be mesmerized either, but they shall recover. Praise God!

Quit your grumbling and get an experience so you can praise God. Many make fun of the work of the Holy Spirit. You can see it in the city papers. God's work cannot be set forth in its true light; it is set forth in a foolish, sensational way, to make people think it is of the devil. "When the Son of man cometh, shall he find faith on the earth?" (Luke 18:8). He will find only a little flock watching for Him. On the Day of Pentecost, Peter did not say, "There is no power here," he said it was the Holy Ghost spoken of by the prophet Joel. They saw the tongues of fire, heard the sound as of a mighty rushing wind. It was the Holy Ghost and He is here tonight. Be careful how you speak against Him. He is in this healing and in the tongues. There is great power among the people, giving the last warning before Jesus comes.

God help us as never before to see Jesus in the power of His blood. Let us give Jesus the preeminence; let us preach Jesus and the Resurrection. Show He is coming by the signs, the power to deliver the people. You know He is coming. Show the signs and you won't have to do much preaching. The people will see the miracles and many will be saved. Let us hold up Jesus as never before; let the people see nothing but Jesus and they will soon drop everything unclean and go higher and higher and deeper yet.

May God put His seal upon these truths in our hearts tonight. The crisis is nearer than any one thinks. Hold up Jesus and God will show them the truth. God must show them working through you. Glory to His Name!

Chapter 22

Thou Shalt Die
and Not Live

THUS SAITH THE LORD, SET THINE HOUSE IN ORDER: FOR thou shalt die, and not live (Isaiah 38:1).

My prayer is that the Lord will arrest every sinner who reads these words; that you will take the warning in the text to mean you and take the nearest way to the Cross and throw yourself at the bleeding feet of the dying Lamb of God, and let Him cleanse and wash out all sin and filth from your heart and mind; and let the Lord Jesus come in and take possession of the house, and fill you with his love and presence, and be the keeper of the house, and speak, that you may obey like a dear child. His sheep hear his voice. When he leads they follow.

Jesus has spoken to you many times by his Spirit and told you this world is not your home, and that it is not all of life to live nor all of death to die, but after death comes the judgment.

He has shown you that you are a sinner, lost and undone, that the wrath of God hangs over you. If you die in your sins it will be an awful thing to fall in the hands of the living God.

If you go on in your sins you will be arrested by the Sheriff of heaven and bound hand and foot, and cast into outer darkness, where the inhabitants weep and wail and gnash their teeth. The Lord has told you the time will come when you will cry for mercy. The mercy door will be closed and God will not hear you. He will laugh and mock at your fears and calamity. He will say, "Depart from me, ye cursed, into everlasting fire" (Matthew 25:41), a place prepared for the devil and his angels.

Heaven was prepared for you, but if you are not pure in heart the Pearly Gates will be closed against you; this world will be wrapped in flames, will burn as pitch and tar, and the wicked will be swept off into destruction.

In view of the awful doom the text implies, make the preparation at once. You must die and there is no repentance in the grave. As you go down in death you will rise in the judgment. Death is coming, that awful eternity is before you! Before the sun rises or sets again you may be cold in death and your soul lost.

The Pale Horse

You will soon hear the clatter of the feet of the pale horse and his rider, the monster death, bearing down upon you. You will have a race with the pale horse and he will run you down into the cold, icy River of Death.

The Lord says, "Prepare for death, for thou shalt die." "As I live, saith the Lord God, I have no pleasure in the death of the wicked; but that the wicked turn from his way and live" (Ezekiel 33:11).

You will die soon and meet your God, whether you are ready or not. He will not always chide, neither will He hold his anger forever.

Hear Him call. Seek the Lord while He may be found. Call upon Him while He is near. God has warned you through the rolling thunder, the flashing lightning and cyclone. The voice of God has spoken to you, saying, "Take warning, fly to Christ and seek shelter from the storms of the great Judgment Day."

The Day of His wrath is coming, and who will be able to stand? Every funeral procession you see tells you that you, too, must soon die. Are you ready? When you stood by the bedside of one struggling in death, or looked on the face in the coffin, the Lord said to you, "Prepare for death and follow me."

Every fall you look upon the withered flowers and falling leaves. They tell you of death. Death is written on the breezes. Everything points to death, and shows you that you will soon be laid away in the silent city of the dead and soon be forgotten by the living.

Moaning Winds, Withering Leaves, Fading Flowers

You hear the solemn moaning of the winds through the leafy trees. They say to you: "This world is not your home: you did not come here to stay forever." Seek a home in heaven, a house not built with hands, whose Builder and Maker is God, where you will soon meet all the loved ones, to be forever with the Lord.

When you walk over the withered flowers and faded leaves, and as they rattle beneath your feet, the voice of God speaks to you, saying, "You are passing away, you will soon be lying 'neath the sod and be forgotten." The thoughtless throng will walk over your moldering form and think no more of you than you do of the dead leaves you are crushing beneath your feet.

Dear reader, if you have not given your heart to Jesus, drop on your knees, confess your sins to Him and accept Him as your personal Saviour; never rise till the light of heaven shines down in your soul and you know you are saved. If you do not, you will soon find yourself swept out on the shores of eternity, lost, lost forever!

The Great Judgment Morning

I dreamed that the Great Judgment morning
    Had dawned, and the trumpet had blown:
I dreamed that the nations had gathered
    To judgment before the White Throne.
From the throne came a bright-shining angel
    And stood on the land and the sea,
And swore with his hand raised to heaven,
    That time was no longer to be.

And, oh, what a weeping and wailing
    When the lost ones were told of their fate:
They cried for the rocks and the mountains,
    They prayed but their prayers were too late.

The rich man was there, but his money
    Had melted and vanished away;
A pauper he stood in the judgment,
    His debts were too heavy to pay.
The great man was there, but his greatness
    When death came was left far behind.
The angel that opened the records
    Not a trace of his greatness could find.

The widow was there and the orphans,
    God heard and remembered their cries;
No sorrow in heaven forever,
    God wiped all the tears from their eyes.
The gambler was there and the drunkard,
    And the man who had sold them the drink,
With the people who gave him the license —
    Together in hell they did sink.

The moral man came to the judgment,
    But his self-righteous rags would not do;
The men who had crucified Jesus
    Had passed off as moral men, too.
The soul that had put off salvation —
    "Not tonight; I'll get saved bye and bye;
No time now to think of religion!"
    At last they had found time to die.

Brief Summary
(Closing Words
by Sister Etter)

New Tabernacle Built—
Work Being Established

SINCE I GOT OUT MY LAST BOOK, "SIGNS AND WONDERS," I HAVE held meetings in a number of places, including some of the largest cities out West. In our meeting at Sidney, Iowa, one of their papers had this to report of the work:

"The crowd of spectators Sunday night was said to have been the largest ever seen at the city park on any occasion. They come back here sick and maimed, on crutches and in wheel chairs, and go away apparently sound and well and shouting hosannas to the Most High. Call it hypnotism or what you will, there is no dodging the fact that Mrs. Etter is exerting a power over these people that passeth common understanding. We give it up; we have no solution."

Also a few words taken from the *Fremont (County) Herald:*

"The big camp meeting is still in progress at the park and is more than ever the main topic of conversation on the streets and in the majority of the homes in Sidney. Each day brings a number of people from a distance, on the train and in autos. The local reporter asked for the names of some of the people who were registered from a distance, but the joke was on her, for there were so many that the paper couldn't print them all. For the first time we can remember, a religious gathering has driven out a good show, and before they went the members of the company, which was booked for the whole week before last at the opera house, went over to the camp meeting to see what had taken their crowds."

These meetings stirred this little town and its surrounding territory as nothing had ever done before. I remember on a Sunday, just as we had dismissed the meeting, the Power of God fell on a little boy with an impediment in speech. He was about twelve years old. He got up and walked back and forth on the platform giving messages in tongues, exhorting the people to get down and pray! pray!! pray!!! He would take his handkerchief and wipe off the perspiration and tears from his face, stamp his little feet and plead with the people to get down and hide away in God and get ready for His coming. In a very short time he had every saint, and nearly all the sinners, down on their knees weeping and calling upon God.

From this little place we went to San Francisco, California. The saints at Salt Lake City, Utah, just a few in number, begged us to get off at their city and hold a meeting. We did so and held a three weeks campaign. God broke through the Mormon ranks. People got saved, healed and baptized. I believe if I could have stayed longer the whole city would have been shaken. On the same mat where prize fights were being staged—stained with blood—sinners were weeping their way through to God, staining it with their tears. Surely this piece of canvas will be a witness for and against some people in the Day of Judgment. At this place the glory of God was seen with the natural eye by about a dozen of the saints. The pastor, an evangelist, myself and workers were among those that saw the wonderful sight—the glory of God like a cloud resting over the meeting.

I am very anxious for the saints and the dear people everywhere to know why we have built the tabernacle....The Lord appeared before me in the night and brought the building before me. He told me to arise and build a house for The Lord. The message and plan came so forcibly before me that I knew it was the voice of God. I rose the next morning, laid the message and plan before my secretary, and told him that we must proceed at once to make arrangements for the building. In about two months time the building was finished. We have a large, neat, comfortable tabernacle. Indianapolis is a large, beautiful, centralized city. A city that is easily accessible to the saints in the North, South, East and West. All those traveling across the continent can conveniently stop off here. The Lord has made it plain that this place is prepared to call the saints together from all parts of the world, to get an especial enduement with power from on high and qualified to do the last work, and get the Last Call, gather in the hungry souls, get them sealed with the seal of the living God and ready for the Rapture.

A brother in Canada wrote me that God showed him that this is to be a lighthouse. That He is going to send the light out all over the world from this place.

God has put His seal on the building and the work in many ways. He has revealed to the saints in different places about establishing a work here. Some have had visions of the building before it was built.

The power and presence of the Lord have been present in a marvelous way from the first meeting, confirming the work with signs and miracles, and in a special manner displaying the supernatural.

The heavenly choir has come forth many times accompanied by heavenly instruments. Angels have been seen, and heard singing by many saints.

The glory of God and Jesus have been seen over the pulpit and all over the tabernacle at times. Last Sunday a brother saw Jesus appear on a throne over the platform. Streams of light and glory were going out from Him all over the building. His face fairly shone while he testified to it. The next night two sisters saw Him at about the same time. One was newly baptized. She saw Him close by her; the other one as He walked across the platform.

The saints are convinced that this is the time for God to do a mighty work.

It depends on the dear ones lending a helping hand everywhere, as we are just building up the work in a new part of the city. We need workers and spiritual help in many ways. Some are talking of moving here. We trust that God will move upon many to come to our help and locate here. He wants to raise up workers that will go out under the anointing and in the unity of the Spirit to carry the work everywhere. We feel and know that this is the Last Call. What we do we must do quickly.

Many People Healed, Saved and Baptized

A Mrs. E.A. Moore of 1212 East Georgia Street was instantly healed of a stroke of paralysis which she took February 24. Her right side and bowels were paralyzed. For some days after she was speechless, too. They brought her to the meeting and had to assist her on the platform. When the prayer of faith was offered for her she got up, walked, and gave praises to God. She demonstrated publicly that she had the right use of her body again. Her neighbors consider it a great miracle. This sister has been well ever since. At another time a colored sister* was brought, in much the same condition. She was prayed for and came in about two weeks later without a sign of lameness.

Saints have come in from all the surrounding states, got what they came for and went back rejoicing. Some of them have come back the second time, bringing others with them.

A brother from Marcellus, Michigan, came down and got spiritually revived. He went back home and brought his mother, wife, two children and some friends to the meeting. These all received their Baptism of the Holy Ghost.

A number of hungry souls came in from Louisville, Kentucky. They also got their baptism.

One man came in from Virginia to get healed of consumption. He got healed and baptized. When he got back home he sent his wife back to be prayed for. She got healed and also received her baptism.

One brother came in from Oklahoma, who had been seeking his baptism for a year. After he was here only a few days he received a marvelous baptism. When he got back home he sent his son, daughter and a friend to Indianapolis. These also received their baptism; only the daughter was a little doubtful if she had received her baptism in its fullness.

As near as I can tell about fifty have already followed Jesus in the ordinance of water baptism at this writing. When the first candidates were baptized in water in the Baptistry, God put his seal on the ceremony in a wonderful way. Messages in tongues with interpretations came forth, and a number of the saints standing close by were slain, and laid like dead under the mighty power of God. A band of angels were seen over the baptistry and heard singing while the ceremony went on.

There are so many people sending in to have us pray over and anoint handkerchiefs that I believe I shall say a few words about this part of my ministry. Like in the days of Paul (see Acts 19:12). God is healing people through pieces of cloth. We have prayed for thousands

---

* Editor's note: Terms used to refer to different races considered accepable in Mrs. Woodworth-Etter's day are offensive and unacceptable today. Inclusion of these terms does not in any way reflect the attitude or policies of Harrison House.

of these cloths and handkerchiefs, and send them out in the Name of Jesus. It is wonderful the reports that come in daily how God heals them. Others get saved and baptized.

A testimony was just handed me from a man from Missouri. In this testimony a consumptive for fifteen years, whose folks had all died with it, was instantly healed when an anointed handkerchief was placed on his body. He has had no more hemorrhages, no coughing, and damp atmospheres have no effect whatsoever upon him any more. He was told by the doctors that he would not live three months if he quit medicine. This is only one out of the many such testimonies that we receive. If the dear saints desire to be helped in this way they should always enclose a self-addressed and stamped envelope for reply. This will save us quite a lot of work and expense.

Now my prayer is that God will greatly bless this little book. They will all be prayed over as they go out in the vineyard. Help us, dear saints, to bring this book of "Holy Ghost Sermons" to many people before Jesus comes. Let us work and sacrifice while we have still an open door. Write for wholesale prices. You can sell them or give them out to hungry souls. What we do for Jesus and His cause must be done very quickly, because the coming of Jesus is right upon us. The Spirit and the bride say come, and let him that is athirst come and whosoever will let him take the water of life freely. Yea, come Lord Jesus. Amen.

Endnotes

Chapter 3

[1]The author at times combines and paraphrases two or more Scriptures rather than quoting directly from the Bible. This is the author's paraphrase of Isaiah 28:11-12 and 1 Corinthians 14:21.

Chapter 5

[1]Author's paraphrase of Isaiah 30:10 and Matthew 15:9.

Chapter 6

[1]Author's paraphrase of Ephesians 4:13; 1 Corinthians 12:7, 11; and Ephesians 4:4-5.

[2]Author's paraphrase of 1 Corinthians 12:1 and Ephesians 4:13.

Chapter 8

[1]Author's paraphrase of Mark 7:7 and Colossians 2:22.

Chapter 9

[1]Author's paraphrase of Isaiah 28:11-12 and 1 Corinthians 14:21.

Chapter 11

[1]Author's paraphrase of 2 Corinthians 6:16 and 1 Corinthians 6:19.

Chapter 16

[1]The author quotes, in order, John 19:5, John 7:46 and Matthew 8:27.

[2]The author here paraphrases, in order, Luke 24:49; Acts 1:8; Matthew 28:18; and Mark 16:15-18.

Chapter 21

[1]The author has paraphrased here, in order, Luke 24:49 and Acts 1:8.

Prayer of Salvation

God loves you—no matter who you are, no matter what your past. God loves you so much that He gave His one and only begotten Son for you. The Bible tells us that "...whoever believes in him shall not perish but have eternal life" (John 3:16 NIV). Jesus laid down His life and rose again so that we could spend eternity with Him in heaven and experience His absolute best on earth. If you would like to receive Jesus into your life, say the following prayer out loud and mean it from your heart.

Heavenly Father, I come to You admitting that I am a sinner. Right now, I choose to turn away from sin, and I ask You to cleanse me of all unrighteousness. I believe that Your Son, Jesus, died on the cross to take away my sins. I also believe that He rose again from the dead so that I might be forgiven of my sins and made righteous through faith in Him. I call upon the name of Jesus Christ to be the Savior and Lord of my life. Jesus, I choose to follow You and ask that You fill me with the power of the Holy Spirit. I declare that right now I am a child of God. I am free from sin and full of the righteousness of God. I am saved in Jesus' name. Amen.

If you prayed this prayer to receive Jesus Christ as your Savior for the first time, please contact us on the web at **www.harrisonhouse.com** to receive a free book.

Or you may write to us at

Harrison House

P.O. Box 35035

Tulsa, Oklahoma 74153

Other Living Classic Books
From Harrison House

Smith Wigglesworth: A Man Who Walked With God

Smith Wigglesworth: A Life Ablaze With the Power of God

Smith Wigglesworth: The Secret of His Power

John G. Lake: Diary of God's General

Questions and Answers on Spiritual Gifts – Howard Carter

His Healing Power – Lilian B. Yeomans

Healing the Sick – T.L. Osborn

Available from your local bookstore
or from **www.harrisonhouse.com**.

Fast. Easy.
Convenient.

For the latest Harrison House product information and author news, look no further than your computer. All the details on our powerful, life-changing products are just a click away. New releases, E-mail subscriptions, Podcasts, testimonies, monthly specials—find it all in one place. Visit harrisonhouse.com today!

harrisonhouse

The Harrison House Vision

Proclaiming the truth and the power
Of the Gospel of Jesus Christ
With excellence;

Challenging Christians to
Live victoriously,
Grow spiritually,
Know God intimately.